# ABITUR Skript



## Englisch

Gymnasium
Baden-Württemberg

STARK

**Bildnachweis:**

Abbildungen Key themes S. 37 ff.: Symbole "Religion" © djdarkflower. Shutterstock; Symbole "Gender" © Albo003. Shutterstock; Symbol "Ethnicity" © grmarc. Shutterstock; Symbol "Family" © 123rf.com; Symbol "Self" © RedKoala. Shutterstock; Symbol "Home" © veronchick84. Shutterstock; Symbol "Violence" © davooda. Shutterstock; Symbol "Guilt" © Leremy. Shutterstock; Symbol "Class" © 123rf.com
Abbildung US-Flagge S. 76: © Rudy Balasko. Shutterstock
Abbildung Esel S. 82: © Kamigami / Dreamstime.com
Abbildung Elefant S. 99: © Kamigami / Dreamstime.com
weitere Abbildungen und grafische Darstellungen: © Redaktion

# Inhalt

## Anglo-American Culture and our Modern World



**Autorin:** Sonja Corleis

# Vorwort

Liebe Schülerinnen und Schüler,

dieses handliche Skript widmet sich den für Ihre Abiturprüfung wesentlichen Inhalten. Es behandelt das aktuelle **Schwerpunktthema** sowie weitere **landeskundliche Bereiche**, die für Ihre **Englisch**-Prüfung in Baden-Württemberg relevant sind.
In seiner klaren Struktur und Fokussierung eignet sich dieses Skript besonders zur Auffrischung und Wiederholung des Prüfungsstoffs kurz vor dem Abitur:

- In den Abschnitten zu ***Crooked Letter, Crooked Letter*** und ***Gran Torino*** werden die wichtigsten Informationen zu Roman und Film in übersichtlicher und prägnanter Form zusammengefasst.
- Der anschließende Abschnitt widmet sich Hauptaspekten des Schwerpunktthemas „**The Ambiguity of Belonging**“ und ihrer Bedeutung für Roman und Film. Hier finden Sie wichtige Interpretationsansätze, die Ihnen bei der Beantwortung von möglichen Prüfungsfragen helfen können.
- Zahlreiche **Schaubilder** fassen die Inhalte übersichtlich zusammen und erleichtern so das Lernen. Darüber hinaus wird mit Originalzitaten aus Roman und Film gearbeitet. Diese dienen als konkrete **Beispiele** für abstrakte Inhalte und weisen Sie auf entscheidende Roman- und Filmstellen hin.
- Zu Beginn des Kapitels „**Anglo-American Culture and our Modern World**“ finden Sie **Mindmaps** zu den abiturrelevanten Themen **USA**, **UK** und **Challenges of our modern world**. Die in den Mindmaps vorkommenden Begriffe werden im anschließenden Glossar kurz und prägnant erklärt.

Viel Erfolg beim Lernen mit diesem Buch und im Abitur!

Sonja Corleis

Sonja Corleis

# *Crooked Letter, Crooked Letter*

In ⇒ **The Ambiguity of Belonging**, you will find more information on the "Schwerpunktthema" and how it links with the novel *Crooked Letter, Crooked Letter* and the film *Gran Torino*.

## 1 Key facts about the novel

- **author:** Tom Franklin, *1963 in Alabama (American South), according to Franklin, *Crooked Letter, Crooked Letter* is partly autobiographical
- **year of publication:** 2010
- **genre:** mixture of **Southern literature** (writing about the American South)/**Southern Gothic** (gloomy moods, dilapidated buildings, bleak landscapes, unlucky and strange characters), **crime novel** (crimes, suspects, suspense, detective, red herrings), **coming-of-age story** (protagonists grow from teenagers to adults)
- **narrative perspective:** third-person narrator with limited point of view → Larry's and Silas's alternating perspectives contribute to the creation of suspense as truth is only gradually revealed
- **structure:** chapters with alternating viewpoints, unchronological presentation of events (mixture of past and present)

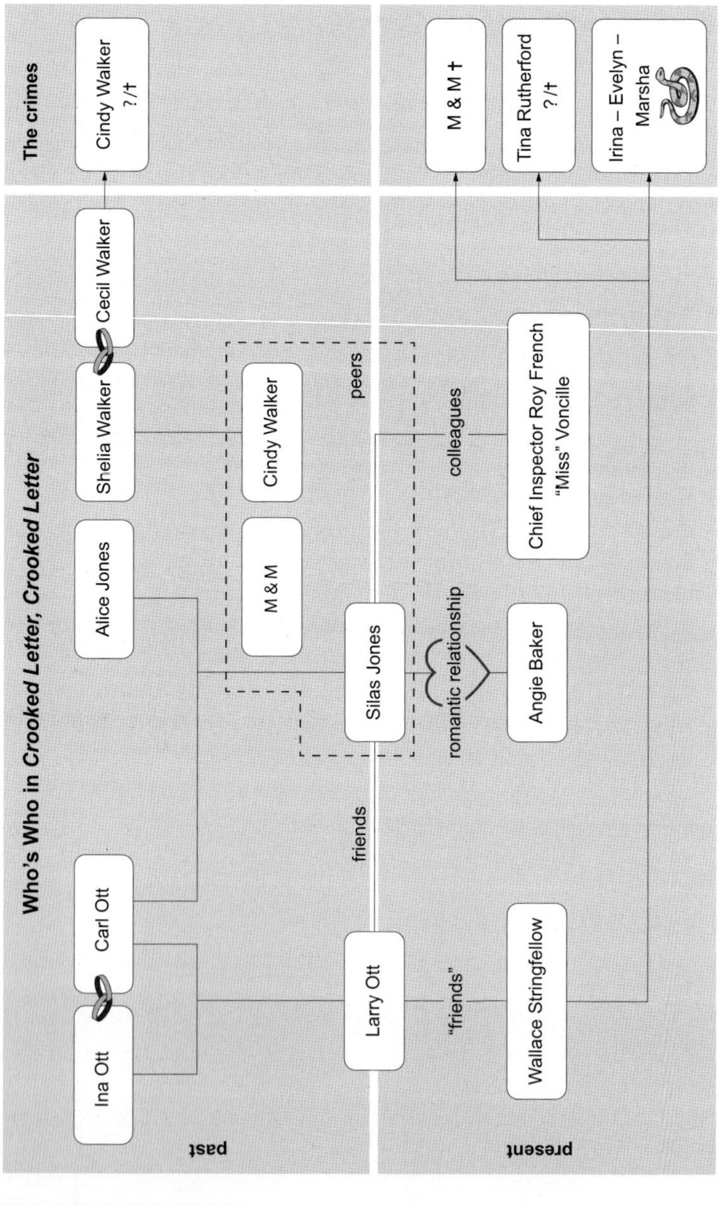
Who's Who in Crooked Letter, Crooked Letter
The crimes
past
present
Ina Ott
Carl Ott
Alice Jones
Shelia Walker
Cecil Walker
Cindy Walker ?/†
M & M
Cindy Walker
peers
Larry Ott
friends
Silas Jones
romantic relationship
colleagues
"friends"
Wallace Stringfellow
Angie Baker
Chief Inspector Roy French
"Miss" Voncille
M & M †
Tina Rutherford ?/†
Irina – Evelyn – Marsha

## 2 Content and structure

In the novel, the events are described in unchronological order and from the alternating viewpoints of Larry and Silas. In the grey bar at the beginning of each chapter, you can see whether a chapter is set in the present (after Tina Rutherford's disappearance) or in the past, and whether it is narrated from Larry's or Silas's view.

| Chapter 1 | present | Larry |
|---|---|---|

- 19-year-old Tina Rutherford missing, Larry Ott suspect
- Larry's daily routine: lives alone on a farm on the outskirts of Chabot, rural Mississippi, works as mechanic in garage with hardly any customers
- Larry shot in his home by someone wearing Larry's own zombie mask

| Chapter 2 | present | Silas |
|---|---|---|

- Constable Silas "32" Jones finds his old classmate "M & M"'s decomposed body
- Silas investigates a snake in Irina Mott and her flatmates' mailbox
- Angie calls Silas from Larry's place, has found wounded Larry

| Chapter 3 | past: March 1979 | Larry |
|---|---|---|

- Carl Ott driving teenage son Larry to school and giving a lift to Alice and Silas Jones
- Ina Ott, Larry's mother, suspicious of Alice and Silas, gives coats to them, but prevents further car rides
- Larry remembers incident when he tried to gain his classmates' respect by racially insulting a black girl
- Larry meets Silas in the forest, lets him borrow his father's rifle

| Chapter 4 | present | Silas |
|---|---|---|

- Silas drives to Larry's house, investigates the crime scene and remembers their childhood together
- Silas finds message Larry left on his answering machine that he needs to tell him something important

| Chapter 5 | past: 1979 | Larry |
|---|---|---|

- secret friendship between Larry and Silas
- boys watch Cindy Walker sunbathing; Silas intervenes when Cindy's stepfather Cecil and Carl Ott molest her
- Carl urges Silas and Larry to fight over his rifle, end of their friendship when Larry, who is about to lose, calls Silas a "nigger"

| Chapter 6 | present – past | Silas |
|---|---|---|

- further investigations of Larry's garage and house
- Silas feeds Ina Ott's chickens
- on old photo, Silas recognises his mother Alice (Otts' maid before becoming pregnant and moving to Chicago)
- flashback: Silas's earlier childhood and youth in Chicago; moves with his mother to Chabot, Mississippi

| Chapter 7 | past: 1982 (and the following years) | Larry |
|---|---|---|

- 16-year-old Larry has a date with Cindy Walker
- Cindy tells Larry that date was only an excuse to get away from home to meet her secret boyfriend
- Larry drives to the drive-in cinema alone
- Cindy never seen again and Larry believed to be her killer ("Scary Larry")
- Larry joins the army, but moves back to Chabot after his father's death to care for his ill mother

| Chapter 8 | present – past | Silas |
|---|---|---|

- Silas tells Angie about his former friendship with Larry
- Silas visits unconscious Larry in hospital and Larry's mother in nursing home
- Silas's sudden realisation that Carl was his father, too
- Silas stops Wallace Stringfellow, who is riding his four-wheeler on Rutherford land, and warns him off trespassing, drunk driving and littering
- Silas finds dead body in shack on the Ott property where he used to live with his mother

| Chapter 9 | past | Larry |
|---|---|---|

- Larry uses his zombie mask to scare away a young intruder
- ten years later, the same boy, Wallace Stringfellow, pretends to be a cable TV salesman in order to get to know Larry
- from then on frequent visits and gradually developing "friendship"
- argument when Wallace insists on learning more about Larry raping and killing Cindy Walker

| Chapter 10 | present – past | Silas |
|---|---|---|

- Silas takes over nightshifts at hospital at unconscious Larry's bed-side
- Silas also continues to visit Ina in nursing home and to feed her chickens
- Silas recalls being a baseball star and having an affair with Cindy Walker, finally confesses the truth to Angie
- Larry wakes up

| Chapter 11 | present | Larry |
|---|---|---|

- Larry waking up in hospital manacled to bed
- Sheriff Lolly and Chief French almost force Larry into confessing

| Chapter 12 | present | Silas |
|---|---|---|

- Silas admits to Lolly, French and Larry that he was the last one to see Cindy
- Irina flirts with Silas and tells him about Wallace Stringfellow, who might have put the snake into the mailbox

| Chapter 13 | present – past | Larry |
|---|---|---|

- still in hospital, Larry remembers his past
- conclusion that Wallace killed Tina Rutherford

| Chapter 14 | present | Silas |
|---|---|---|

- Silas drives to Wallace Stringfellow to investigate case of snake in the mailbox
- Silas attacked by Wallace's dog and threatened by one of his snakes

| Chapter 15 | present | Larry |
|---|---|---|

- Larry tells Chief French everything he knows about Wallace
- Silas brought into Larry's hospital room

| Chapter 16 | present | Silas |
|---|---|---|

- Silas celebrated as local hero who brought down Tina Rutherford's murderer Wallace, who shot himself when confronted by the police
- Silas tells Larry that Carl was the dad of both of them
- Larry asks to be put into another room

| Chapter 17 | present | Larry |
|---|---|---|

- Wallace connected to Rutherford case, shooting Larry and probably killing M&M
- Larry's name cleared
- Silas leaves hospital and promises to visit Larry

| Chapter 18 | present | Silas |
|---|---|---|

- Silas tells the whole truth to a reporter
- Silas visits Larry who is still angry at him for hiding the truth for so long
- Silas makes further amends: visits to Ina Ott, cleaning Larry's house with Angie and returning Carl Ott's rifle

| Chapter 19 | present | Larry and Silas |
|---|---|---|

- Larry remains silent during Silas's frequent visits
- Silas takes Larry home from hospital in his old car, asks him to repair it and Larry finally agrees

## Timeline

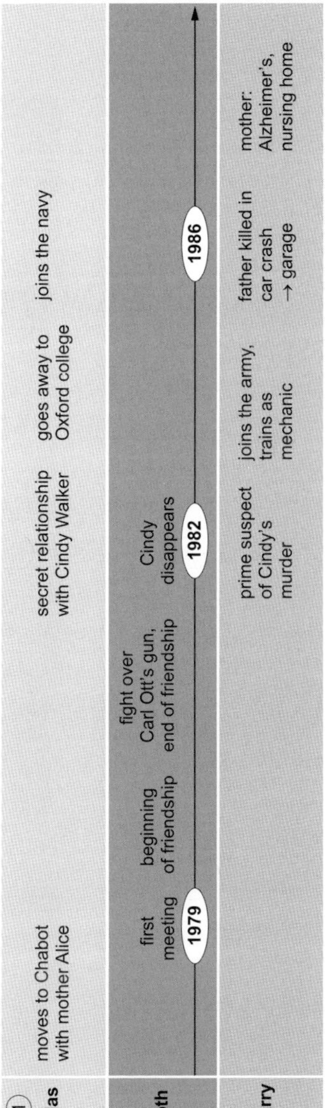
1
Silas
both
Larry
moves to Chabot with mother Alice
first meeting
1979
beginning of friendship
fight over Carl Ott's gun, end of friendship
secret relationship with Cindy Walker
Cindy disappears
1982
prime suspect of Cindy's murder
goes away to Oxford college
joins the army, trains as mechanic
joins the navy
1986
father killed in car crash → garage
mother: Alzheimer's, nursing home

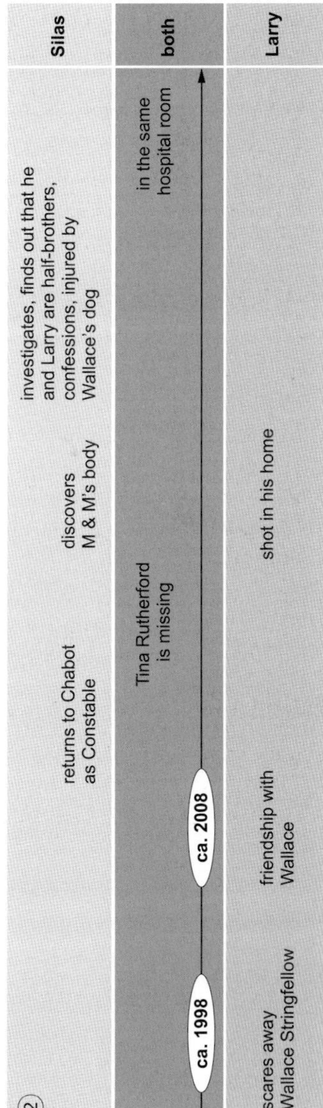
2
Silas
both
Larry
…
ca. 1998
scares away Wallace Stringfellow
ca. 2008
friendship with Wallace
returns to Chabot as Constable
Tina Rutherford is missing
discovers M & M's body
shot in his home
investigates, finds out that he and Larry are half-brothers, confessions, injured by Wallace's dog
in the same hospital room

# 3 Characters

## Main characters

### Larry Ott

**nickname:** Scary Larry

**age:** 41

**ethnicity:** Caucasian

**job:** mechanic, runs the garage of his late father

**interests:** books (esp. horror stories), animals and nature

**character traits:** not manly enough (according to his father), insecure, shy, polite and kind, loyal

**relationship with other characters:** bullied by his peers, misunderstood and mistreated by his father, close to his mother, former friendship with Silas Jones, isolated and ostracised as potential murderer, as town outcast only friend Wallace Stringfellow

### Silas Jones

**nickname:** 32 (number as a baseball player)

**ethnicity:** African American

**job:** police constable in Chabot

**interests:** baseball

**character traits:** proud as a young boy, athletic, outspoken, but tries to evade responsibility for his acts, shows courage when he finally confesses and exonerates Larry, feeling of duty towards Larry (bad conscience)

**relationship with other characters:** mother Alice Jones, father Carl Ott (which he did not know), former friendship with Larry (his half-brother), former interracial relationship with Cindy Walker, girlfriend Angie, respected in town

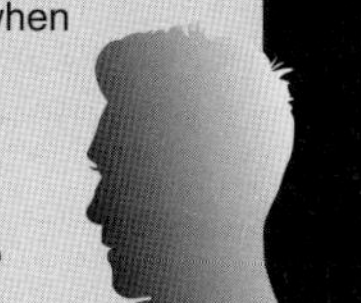

### Carl Ott

**death:** died in car accident (drunk driving, alcoholic)

**ethnicity:** Caucasian

**job:** mechanic

**character traits:** cruel, abusive, sadistic, redneck, racist

**relationship with other characters:** married to Ina, son Larry (whom he mistreats and despises), affair with former housemaid Alice Jones, illegitimate son Silas (does not acknowledge him), friendship with Cecil Walker and other rednecks

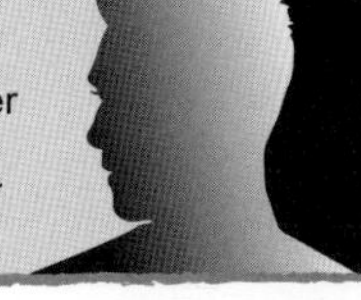

## Ina Ott

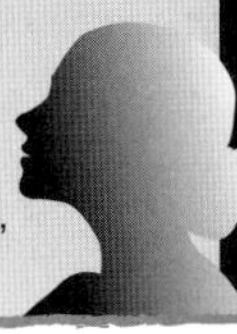

**state of health:** lives in a nursing home, suffers from Alzheimer's disease

**ethnicity:** Caucasian

**interests:** chickens, church, her son Larry

**character traits:** sensitive and compassionate, religious

**relationship with other characters:** husband Carl (Ina sometimes outspoken against generally dominant Carl), emotionally attached to her son Larry

## Alice Jones

**ethnicity:** African American

**job:** Otts' maid when Larry was born, later two jobs and cleaning work to care for her son

**character traits:** determined, strong-willed, proud, protective of her son

**relationship with other characters:** single mother to Silas (after affair with employer Carl Ott), return from Chicago to Chabot after relationship with criminal boyfriend ended, secretly supported by Carl (lives in cabin in the woods)

## Cindy Walker

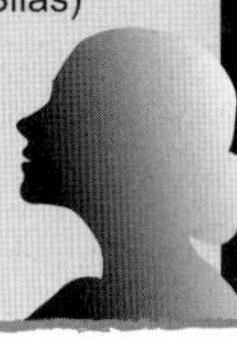

**ethnicity:** Caucasian

**interests:** musicals, boys, her looks, baseball (because of Silas)

**character traits:** rebellious, manipulative

**relationship with other characters:** idolised by many of her peers, dysfunctional family (stepfather Cecil molests and probably kills her), secret relationship with Silas, takes advantage of Larry's admiration for her

## Cecil Walker

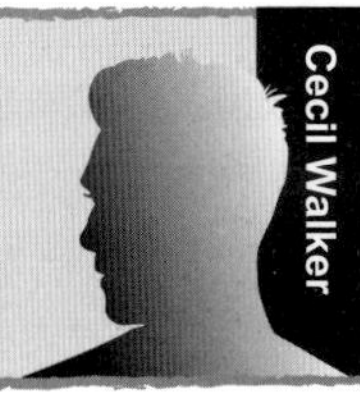

**ethnicity:** Caucasian

**character traits:** racist, abusive

**relationship with other characters:** Carl Ott's drinking buddy, Cindy Walker's stepfather (molests and behaves sexually inappropriate towards her, probably her killer)

**Wallace Stringfellow**

**ethnicity:** Caucasian
**interests:** snakes, dogs, guns, alcohol, cannabis
**social background:** poor, criminal
**character traits:** violent, psychotic, needy, affectionate
**relationship with other characters:** friendship with Larry (cruelly fascinated by his alleged criminal background), violent relationship with women (kills Tina Rutherford)

### Minor characters

- **Angie Baker:** Silas Jones's girlfriend, EMT (emergency medical technician), African American, compassionate and outspoken
- **Chief Roy French:** district chief investigator, Silas's boss, Caucasian, cynical
- "**Miss**" **Voncille:** town clerk and police dispatcher
- **Irina Mott, Evelyn and Marsha:** flatmates on "White Trash Avenue", find a snake in their mailbox
- **Tina Rutherford:** daughter of the very wealthy Rutherford Mill's owner, gone missing at the age of 19, found murdered in old cabin in the woods

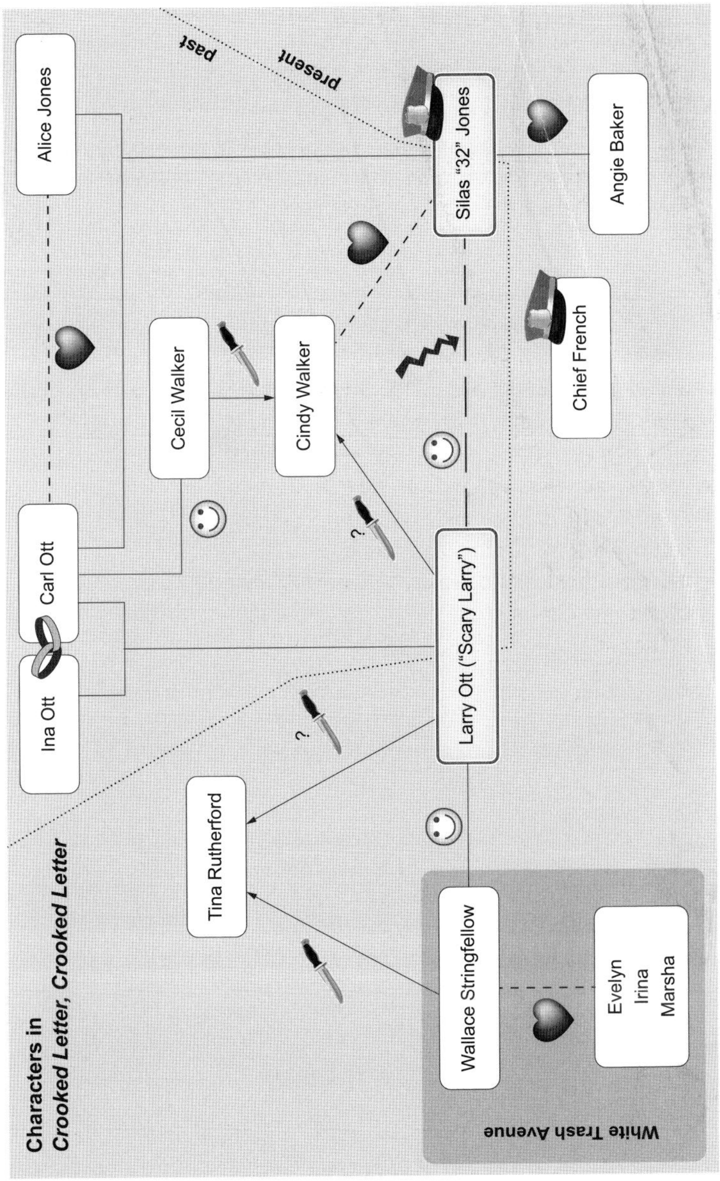
Characters in
*Crooked Letter, Crooked Letter*
Alice Jones
past
present
Silas "32" Jones
Angie Baker
Cecil Walker
Cindy Walker
Chief French
Carl Ott
Ina Ott
Larry Ott ("Scary Larry")
Tina Rutherford
Wallace Stringfellow
Evelyn
Irina
Marsha
White Trash Avenue

## 4 Interpretation of the title

- named after how children in the South are taught to spell Mississippi: "M – I – crooked letter – crooked letter – I – crooked letter – crooked letter – I – humpback – humpback – I" (crooked letter = S)
- the American South: known for conservative political attitudes, sweltering climate, rundown places, etc.

- Mississippi River: does not play any dominant role, but symbolic of the meandering of the story, its curves, developing slowly, going back a bit and forward again
- "crooked" also means "dishonest"; many dishonest characters in the story:
  - Larry using Cindy to become more popular and impress his parents
  - Silas not declaring Larry's innocence
  - Carl not admitting his fatherhood of Silas
  - Cindy using Larry to secretly meet Silas
  - Wallace lying, e. g. about his job

# 5 Motifs and symbols

## The zombie mask

- **occurrence in the story:** ordered by teenager Larry, who brought it to school and was famous for one day and even invited to Halloween party; later used by Larry to scare away intruder (Wallace); stolen by Wallace who has it on when shooting Larry; convicts Wallace when Silas finds it at his place
- **symbolism:** hidden identity, being someone else, power, popularity

**Examples**

- **Chapter 1, p. 8[1]:** "Larry felt a strange forgiveness for him because all monsters were misunderstood." (adult Larry attacked by Wallace who is wearing Larry's zombie mask)
- **Chapter 8, p. 165:** "Larry stood in the floodlight for a long time. Figuring it out. The mask deflated under his arm. Finally he turned and walked down the dirt road toward the paved one. He paused at the road in his whipping sheet and waited [...] waited a long time [...] In case anybody glanced over and happened to notice him and yell, 'Hey, look! It's Larry! Come back! Join the party!' No one did, including Silas, including Cindy." (Larry as a teenager, invited to Halloween party because of his zombie mask, "popular for one day")

1 All chapters and pages refer to: Tom Franklin, *Crooked Letter, Crooked Letter.* Pan Books: London, Basingstoke and Oxford, 2014.

## Books

- **occurrence in the story:** Larry has always been an avid reader (much to his father's displeasure), special fan of Stephen King's horror stories, tries to interest Silas in the stories as well; as an adult books are Larry's only companions
- **symbolism:** escape, Larry's status as an outsider (vs. "cool", athletically inclined boys), Larry seen as weak and girlish, education/Larry's field of expertise

### Examples

- **Chapter 2, p. 23:** "'I was in school with him's all. Knew him a little way back when.' 'He didn't play ball, did he?' Voncille asked. 'Naw. Just read books.' 'Horror books,' French said. 'His house is full of em.'" (conversation between adult Silas and colleagues about Larry and his love of horror books) ⇒ **status as an outsider**
- **Chapter 5, p. 82:** "He went down the hall toward his room but heard his father call, 'Hey, boy?' He hurried back. 'Yes, sir?' 'You stay outside today. Cut the grass.' Which meant *Don't read all day.*" (Carl wanting young Larry to behave more like a "real boy") ⇒ **Larry seen as weak and girlish**
- **Chapter 7, p. 155:** "Larry never returned to school, the weeks stretching into months, and when even the most fervent optimists were beginning to doubt she'd run away, after Silas had left for Oxford, Larry spent his hours in his room, reading." (after Cindy's disappearance) ⇒ **escape**
- **Chapter 12, p. 251:** "'Did you bring me *Night Shift*?' The men followed his eyes to the book on the table between the beds. […] 'Did you ever read it?' 'Yeah.' 'You like it?' 'No,' he said. […] He wanted to say how Larry's versions, way back when, were better, but French cleared his throat." (Larry in hospital, Silas remembering the past and Larry's love of books) ⇒ **education/Larry's field of expertise**

## Snakes

- **occurrence in the story:** Larry loves snakes; Wallace collects them and places one in Irina's mailbox; Silas is almost killed by a snake in Wallace's house
- **symbolism:** devilish temptation to see the truth; foreboding something bad; crookedness; in Larry's case also his expertise on nature (friendship with Silas, status as an oddball, common ground with Wallace)

**Examples**

- **Chapter 2, p. 33:** "'Yall got any idea who might have done this?' he asked. The women frowning at one another [...]" (Silas investigating snake in the mailbox) ⇒ **foreboding**
- **Chapter 4, pp. 69/70:** "They'd [...] caught lizards – anoles, Larry had called them. Then quickly added, 'But some people call em "lizards," too.'" (Silas remembering him and Larry as friends) ⇒ **Larry's expertise on nature**
- **Chapter 12, pp. 261/262:** "'So this guy. You think he mailed the snake?' 'Maybe. She admitted she left her other place cause of him. He kept riding by. Calling.' 'What's his name?' 'Wallace. Wallace Stringfellow. Lives over on past the catfish farm.' He felt his pocket for a pen and scribbled the name on a napkin, stuffed it in his jeans pocket. It rang a dim bell. That guy on the four-wheeler? With the pillowcase. Wasn't that his name? Didn't Larry once say a good way to carry snakes was in a pillowcase?" (conversation between Silas and Irina Mott, threads gradually connecting and pointing towards Wallace as the culprit) ⇒ **foreboding**
- **Chapter 14, pp. 278/279:** "Silas went around the counter into the kitchen, scanning the room, the aquariums between the two of them, and bent, his face inches from a fat cottonmouth, lying like a big burnt arm. He could see its frozen frown, the pits under its slit eyes, flicking tongue the only sign it was alive." (Silas investigating at Wallace's house) ⇒ **foreboding**

### Carl Ott's rifle

- **occurrence in the story:** Larry borrows it from his father and shows it to Silas (beginning of their friendship), later lends it to Silas ("buying" his friendship); Carl makes Larry and Silas fight over the gun (end of friendship), Silas wins the gun, in the end Silas returns the gun to Larry's home (kind of apology); Larry as a suspect not allowed to own guns; Wallace obsessed with guns, gives Larry a gun for Christmas
- **symbolism:** manliness, fatherhood, power, beginning/end/renewal of friendship

**Examples**

- **Chapter 5, p. 103:** "'Let me-me-me-me-me uh-uh-up,' Larry said again, louder, a note of panic. Silas tightened his grip. 'La-la-la-la-listen at the little stuttering baby,' Carl said. 'Quit it Sssssilas!' he cried. 'Ple-ple-ple-please.' Silas held on. 'You,' Larry burbled, 'you n-n-n-nigger.' Silas let him go and rose. [...] Silas looked different than Larry had ever seen him. His eyes now flashed the same fierceness the other black boys at school had" (Silas and Larry fighting for Carl Ott's rifle) ⇒ **power; end of friendship**

- **Chapter 18, pp. 304/305:** "For a moment he held the old rifle, which Angie had helped him clean that morning. It seemed lighter than it used to. [...] Holding it for a moment he was a boy again, the world the world it had been a long time ago, a world full of unknowns, a world full of future and possibility, but then he reached and set the rifle down stock first in the green velvet oval and fit its barrel in its green velvet groove and it stood there, a thing returned to its rightful place. Silas inhaled, a man now, full of unknowns yet, but, maybe, with some future still ahead. Some possibility. He looked a moment longer, then turned and went up the hall to where his girl was standing up, pushing her hands into the small of her back." (Silas and Angie preparing Larry's house for his return from hospital) ⇒ **renewal of friendship**

### Mailboxes

- **occurrence in the story:** Larry's mailbox regularly the target of wanton destruction, manifesting his ostracism; rattlesnake in Irina's mailbox finally leads to Wallace Stringfellow
- **symbolism:** connection of individual to outside world (or lack thereof)

**Examples**

- **Chapter 2, pp. 28/29:** "'You need to get over to Fourteenth and West. It's a rattlesnake in somebody's mailbox. [...] It being, you know, in the box? That makes it a federal crime.'" (Silas sent to investigate snake in Irina Mott's mailbox)
- **Chapter 13, p. 264:** "Larry was flicking through channels on cable television, thinking of his mailbox. Over the years he'd repaired it half a dozen times, mornings as he left for work discovering it by the highway, askew on its post or the whole thing knocked down and splayed in the mud, sometimes magazines fluttering over the road like chickens on the loose. Once the box and post missing altogether. He knew about this, how teenagers rode along, hanging out car windows with baseball bats. Knowing it happened to others should've been a comfort, but as he'd driven on to his shop those days, he'd noticed other mailboxes still standing and known that he alone had been targeted." (Larry in hospital remembering acts of vandalism against his mailbox)

### Chickens

- **occurrence in the story:** Larry cares for his mother's chickens, even builds a contraption to give them fresh grass each day; when Larry is in hospital, Silas feeds the chickens for him
- **symbolism:** Larry's devotion and loyalty as a son; kindness towards animals; Silas's cowardice and later redemption

**Examples**

- **Chapter 6, p. 111:** "He noticed the wheels on the back of the cage, frowned as he walked its width and turned and walked, the chickens shadowing him, its length. He toed the trailer hitch. Why would Larry want wheels on his pen? He looked out over the field and saw several brownish spots in the otherwise bright green weeds and wildflowers, each spot the size of the cage beside him. Walking, he imagined Larry tractoring the cage over the land, the chickens fluttering along inside." (Silas discovering Larry's mobile contraption for the chicken pen) ⇒ **Larry's devotion and loyalty as a son, kindness towards animals**
- **Chapter 10, p. 237:** "*What's missing out of you, Silas?* Courage, he thought. No wonder he felt at ease among these damn chickens." (Silas feeling bad for not telling the truth about the night of Cindy's disappearance, remembering his mother's rebuke) ⇒ **cowardice**

## Coats and gloves

- **occurrence in the story:** Ina Ott gives coats to Alice and Silas when they first move to Mississippi, but does not want them to ride in Carl's car to school; Larry leaves gloves for Silas in the forest
- **symbolism:** poverty of Silas and his mother; Alice's affair with Carl; Alice's humiliation; unbalanced friendship between Silas and Larry; Silas's pride

**Examples**

- **Chapter 3, p. 39:** "Larry stuck out his calfskin glove. Silas's slender brown hand was bare, and despite the quick soul shake it gave, Larry felt how cold his skin was. If he gave him one of his gloves, they could each have one warm hand. He wanted to do this, but how?" (Larry's and Silas's first meeting in Carl Ott's car)
- **Chapter 3, p. 43:** "'You've never minded,' Larry's mother said to Alice, looking hard at her, 'using other people's things.'" (Ina Ott giving coats to Silas and Alice, implicitly criticising her for her affair with Carl)
- **Chapter 3, p. 63:** "The last thing he did was pull at the fingers of his gloves, removing the left one, the right, and erect a stick the shape of a Y in the cold mulch beneath the leaves. On each peg he left a glove." (Larry leaving gloves in the forest for Silas)

# *Gran Torino*

## 1 Key facts about the movie

- **screenplay:** written by Nick Schenk
- **director and producer:** Clint Eastwood (also stars as main character)
- **release date:** 2008 / 2009
- **genre: modern-day Western** (plot centring on "lone Cowboy" / hero Walt who takes the law into his own hands), **action movie** (scenes of violence and fighting), **psychological drama** (focus on psychological conflicts, fraught relationships, heartbreaking ending)
- **setting:** Detroit area, Michigan
- **structure:** frame of two funerals (Dorothy and Walt Kowalski), development of Walt and Thao's friendship, escalation of gang violence, Thao's process of growing up

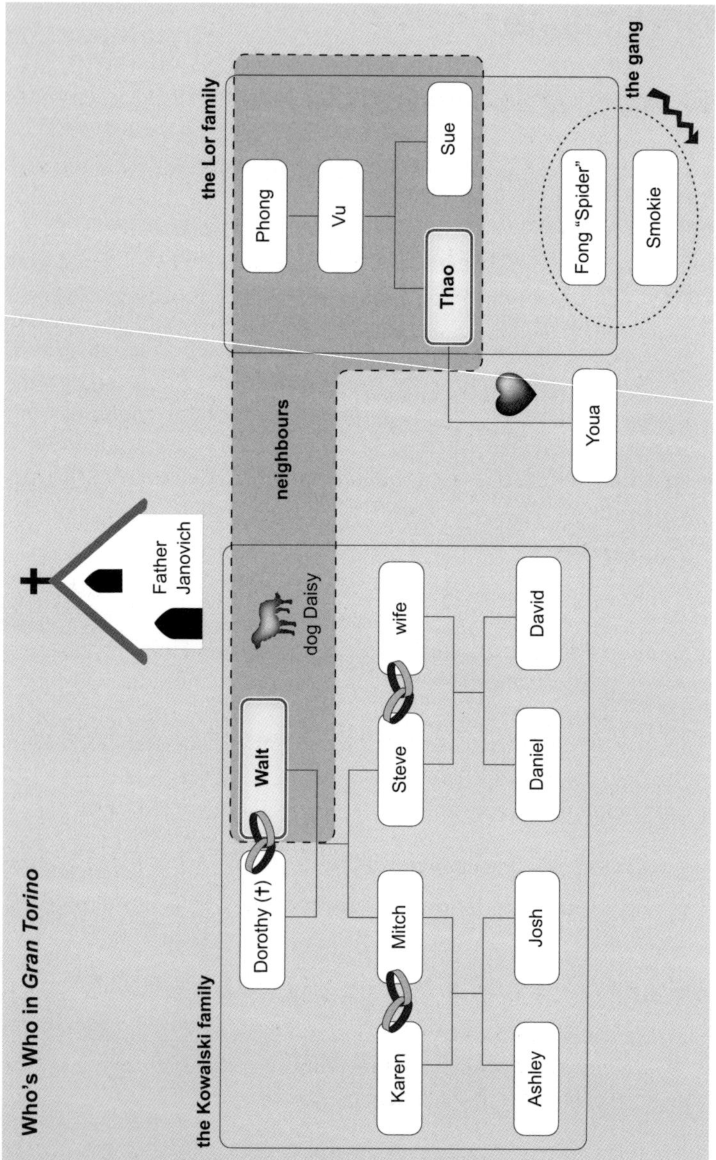
Who's Who in *Gran Torino*
Father Janovich
the Kowalski family
Dorothy (†)
Walt
dog Daisy
Karen
Mitch
Steve
wife
Ashley
Josh
Daniel
David
neighbours
the Lor family
Phong
Vu
Thao
Sue
Youa
Fong "Spider"
Smokie
the gang

# 2 Content and structure

**Setting 1: At the church (ca. 00:45–03:43)[2]**

- Dorothy Kowalski's funeral service
- widower Walt is visibly upset about family's behaviour and Father Janovich's shallow sermon

**Setting 2: In Walt's house/Outside Walt's house (ca. 03:44–09:44)**

- Walt's grandsons find memorabilia of Korean war in Walt's cellar
- Walt's granddaughter Ashley bluntly asks him to inherit 1972 Gran Torino Sport
- traditional Hmong birth ceremony at Walt's neighbours' house
- Father Janovich wants Walt to go to confession, Walt rejects this

**Setting 3: Inside the Lors' house (ca. 09:45–11:05)**

- Thao's grandmother Phong complains about Thao not being "the man of the house"

**Setting 4: On the porches (ca. 11:06–12:40)**

- Walt and Phong suspiciously eye each other from their porches
- Walt refuses Father Janovich's offer for confession again

**Setting 5: In the street (ca. 12:41–15:08)**

- Hispanic gang bullies Thao
- cousin Spider and his gang help Thao, want him to join them

**Setting 6: In the Lors' garden (ca. 15:09–17:22)**

- gang pressures Thao into joining them and stealing Walt's Gran Torino

**Setting 7: At a bar (ca. 17:23–20:04)**

- Father Janovich's next attempt to talk to Walt
- Walt mentions experiences on the Korean battlefield, implying that he knows more about death than the young priest

2 Times refer to the DVD version of *Gran Torino* and may vary slightly when played on different devices.

**Setting 8:** **In Walt's house and garage (ca. 20:05–21:17)**

- Thao's attempt to steal the Gran Torino thwarted by Walt pointing a gun at him

**Setting 9:** **In Walt's garage and house (ca. 21:18–22:27)**

- telephone call by Walt's son Mitch, only interested in football tickets

**Setting 10:** **On Walt's lawn and in the street (ca. 22:28–25:39)**

- Hmong gang harasses Thao
- Walt drives them away by threatening them with rifle

**Setting 11:** **On Walt's porch (ca. 25:40–29:43)**

- Hmong community's presents to Walt for helping Thao
- Sue, Thao's sister, and her mother Vu make Thao apologise to Walt
- Father Janovich's next attempt to talk to Walt

**Setting 12:** **On the sidewalk (ca. 29:44–34:47)**

- Sue and boyfriend Trey harassed by group of African American teenagers
- Walt intervenes, helps Sue and drives her home

**Setting 13:** **In Walt's truck (ca. 34:48–36:48)**

- conversation between Sue and Walt: she tells him about the Hmong

**Setting 14:** **On Walt's porch and in his house (ca. 36:49–41:57)**

- Walt's birthday: Mitch and Karen's presents are only badly veiled attempts to cart Walt off to an old people's home
- Sue invites left alone Walt to a party at their house

**Setting 15:** **The Lors' house (ca. 41:58–51:41)**

- Walt introduced to guests, rituals and traditional food at party
- shaman doctor "reads" Walt quite accurately ("not at peace")
- younger people gathered in the basement of the house, Thao too shy to ask Youa out, Walt provokes him

**Setting 16:** **In front of Walt's house (ca. 51:42–53:47)**

- Thao offers to work for Walt to make up for his attempt to steal Gran Torino

**Setting 17:** **Inside and outside Walt's house (ca. 53:48–58:34)**

- Walt gives Thao only useless tasks
- Thao finally refurbishes houses of the neighbourhood; feels valued
- Walt coughs up blood and rudely sends Thao away

**Setting 18:** **At the doctor (ca. 58:35–59:33)**

- Walt at the doctor's

**Setting 19:** **Walt's house/Mitch's house (ca. 59:34–01:01:00)**

- Walt's attempt to tell Mitch about his bad diagnosis thwarted by his son's indifference

**Setting 20:** **The Lors' and Walt's houses (ca. 01:01:01–01:10:06)**

- Walt helps Thao with repair works and asks for his help in return
- closer relationship between Walt and Thao

**Setting 21:** **At the barber shop (ca. 01:10:07–01:13:18)**

- Walt's attempt to "man Thao up": learning "men's talk" at Martin's barber shop

**Setting 22:** **On a construction site/In a hardware store (ca. 01:13:19–01:16:46)**

- Walt helps Thao get a job on construction site and buys him equipment

**Setting 23:** **In the street (ca. 01:16:47–01:19:29)**

- Spider's gang's assault on Thao

**Setting 24:** **In front of the gang's house (ca. 01:19:30–01:21:23)**

- Walt beats up Smokie and tells him to leave Thao alone

**Setting 25:** **Walt's garden (ca. 01:21:24–01:22:40)**

- Walt, Thao, Sue, Vu and Youa have barbecue
- Walt promises to lend Thao and Youa Gran Torino for first date

**Setting 26:** **The Lors' house (ca. 01:22:41–01:25:40)**

- in revenge for Walt's beating up of Smokie, gang shoots at Lors' house with semi-automatic guns, wounding Thao
- Sue returns home, badly beaten up and raped

**Setting 27:** **Walt's house (ca. 01:25:41–01:29:38)**

- Walt's self-blame for violence
- first open conversation between Walt and Father Janovich

**Setting 28:** **Walt's house (ca. 01:29:39–01:31:11)**

- Thao seeks revenge, but is sent away by Walt

**Setting 29:** **Walt's house, shops and church (ca. 01:31:12–01:34:37)**

- Walt gets his affairs in order: mows his lawn, has a bath, visits the barber's, buys a tailored suit, finally goes to confession (deploring his distanced relationship with his sons)

**Setting 30:** **Walt's house (ca. 01:34:38–01:38:39)**

- Thao locked up in the basement by Walt to prevent him from taking revenge and tarnishing his "pure" soul
- Walt brings dog Daisy to grandmother Phong

**Setting 31:** **In front of the gang's house (ca. 01:38:40–01:43:52)**

- Walt confronts the gang about violence against Sue and her family
- Walt's final sacrifice: provokes the gang into shooting him dead (by taking out his lighter, pretending it to be a gun) in full view of witnesses
- gang members arrested for murder of an unarmed man
- Thao and Sue watch while Walt's body is taken away

**Setting 32:** **In church and at a lawyer's office (ca. 01:43:53–01:46:21)**

- Walt's funeral: Thao and Sue in traditional dress; Father Janovich's personal sermon
- Walt's last will: Thao inherits Gran Torino

**Setting 33:** **At the shore of Lake St. Claire (ca. 01:46:22–01:47:30)**

- Thao driving the Gran Torino with Daisy sitting next to him

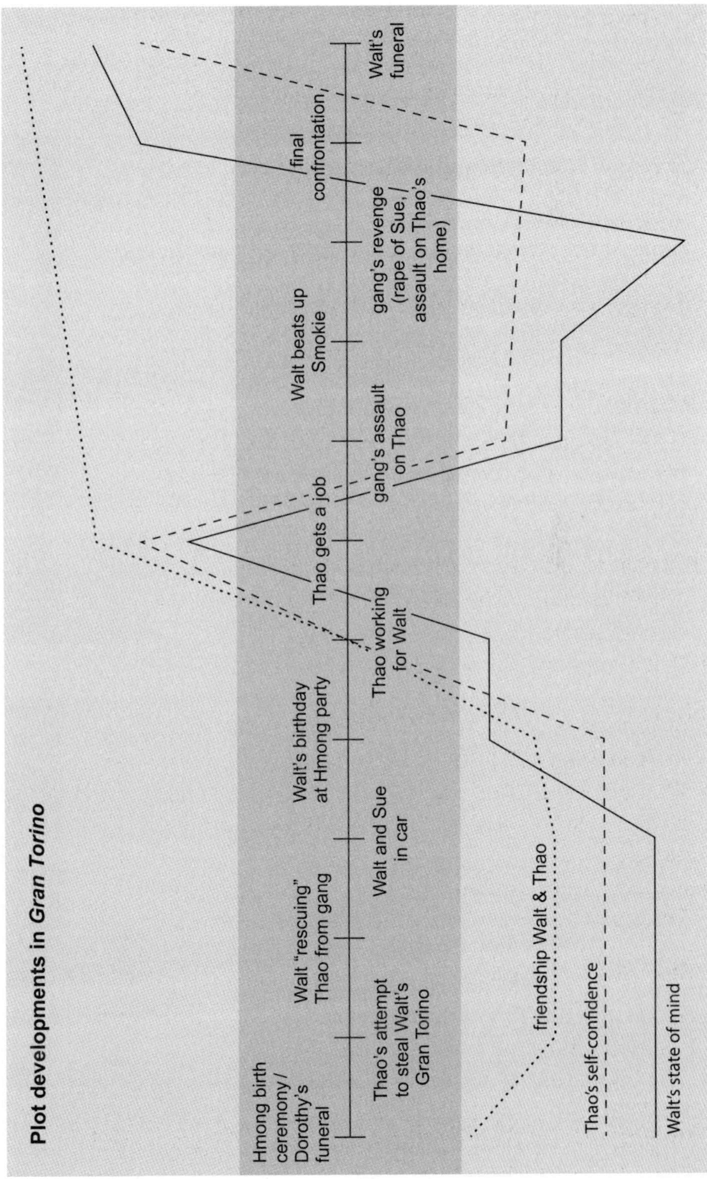


**Plot developments in *Gran Torino***

# 3 Characters

## Main characters

### Walt Kowalski

**nickname:** Wally (by Sue, as a form of endearment)

**age:** in his 70s

**ethnicity:** Caucasian, descendant of Polish immigrants

**health:** suffers from severe illness, probably lung cancer

**job:** Korean War veteran, worked in a Ford factory

**interests:** cars, repairing things, keeping house and garden in order, his dog Daisy, smoking, drinking

**character traits:** self-reliant and determined, conservative and tidy-minded, grumpy, hostile and racist, but also conscience-stricken and lonely

**relationship with other characters:** had a loving marriage with Dorothy (recently deceased), difficult relationship with his sons and their families, "manly" banter with Martin, the barber, Tim, the construction supervisor, and other drinking buddies, gradually develops respect for Father Janovich whom he rejects and ridicules at the beginning, gradual friendship with Thao and Sue, who become like a substitute family to him, feels responsible for them and finally sacrifices his life for their happiness

### Thao Vang Lor

**nickname:** Toad (by Walt who does not make an effort to pronounce his name correctly, first an insult, then almost a term of endearment)

**age:** about 16

**ethnicity:** Hmong

**job:** does not go to school, later gets a job at a construction site

**interests:** cars, handiwork

**character traits:** shy, self-conscious, insecure, gains self-confidence by working and through friendship with Walt

**relationship with other characters:** lives with sister, mother, grandmother, but is not seen as "man of the house", pressured by cousin Fong to join his gang, in love with Youa, torn between two worlds of white America and traditional Hmong culture, gradually becomes friends with Walt and learns a lot from him

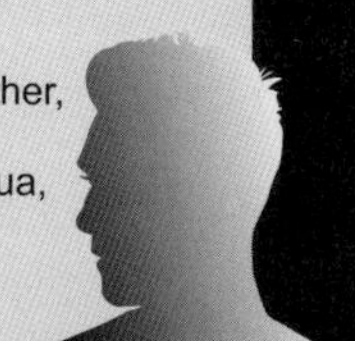

**Sue Lor**

**age:** a little bit older than Thao
**ethnicity:** Hmong
**job:** goes to school /college
**character traits:** self-confident, outspoken, intelligent, witty
**relationship with other characters:** feels responsible for her brother, speaks up against Smokie and Spider, but gets beaten and raped by the gang, sees Walt's good heart beneath his hostile behaviour, well-adapted to American society: white boyfriend Trey

**Father Janovich**

**age:** 27 (according to Walt)
**ethnicity:** Caucasian
**job:** Catholic priest
**interests:** his parish, philosophical questions about life and death
**character traits:** young and inexperienced, persistent, really cares for the people in his parish
**relationship with other characters:** was close to Dorothy Kowalski, learns a lot from Walt and gains his respect

## Minor characters

- **Fong ("Spider") and Smokie:** ringleaders of violent Hmong gang, Fong is Sue's and Thao's cousin
- **Mitch, Karen, Ashley and Josh Kowalski:** Walt's son and his family, difficult relationship with Walt (feel like Walt is never content with and always disappointed in them, but they are rather materialistically interested in Walt themselves)
- **Steve, wife, Daniel and David Kowalski:** Walt's other son and his family, little contact to Walt
- **Martin:** Italian-American barber, Walt's friend
- **Phong Lor:** Thao and Sue's grandmother, suspicious of American culture and rather hostile towards Walt
- **Vu Lor:** Thao and Sue's single mother, does not speak English
- **Youa:** Thao's love interest
- **Trey:** Sue's rather cowardly Caucasian boyfriend

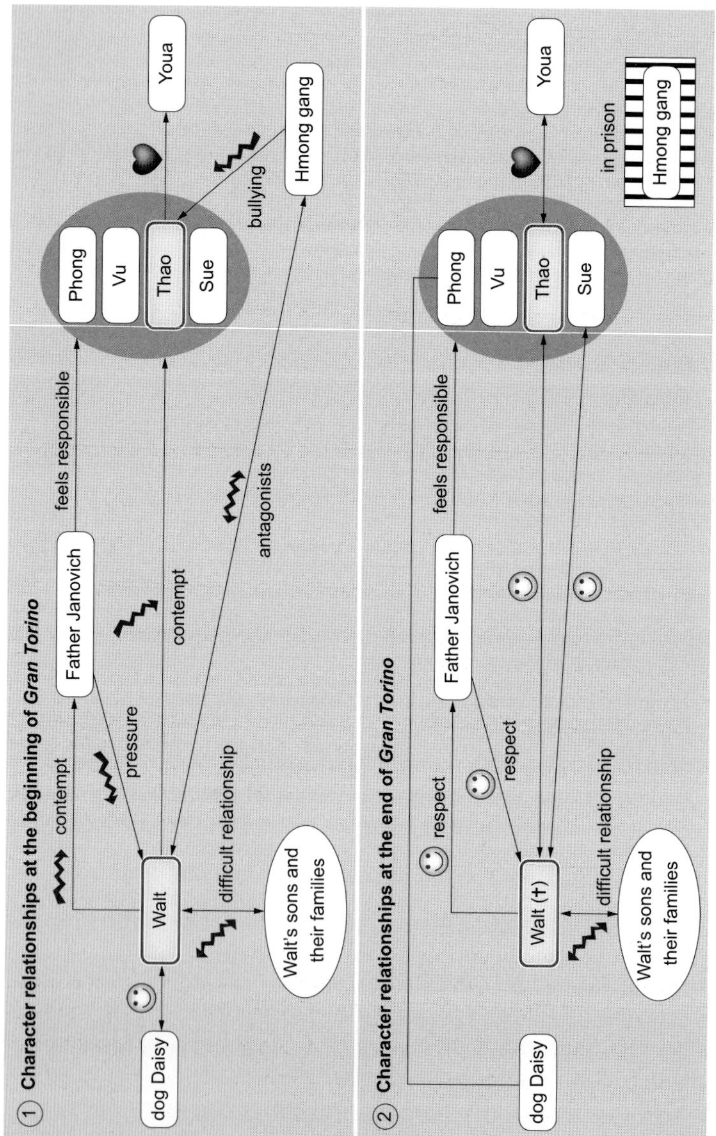
① Character relationships at the beginning of Gran Torino
dog Daisy
Walt
Walt's sons and their families
difficult relationship
contempt
Father Janovich
pressure
feels responsible
contempt
antagonists
Phong
Vu
Thao
Sue
Youa
bullying
Hmong gang
② Character relationships at the end of Gran Torino
dog Daisy
Walt (†)
Walt's sons and their families
difficult relationship
respect
respect
Father Janovich
feels responsible
Phong
Vu
Thao
Sue
Youa
in prison
Hmong gang

# 4 Motifs and symbols

## Gran Torino

- **importance in the film:** Walt's prized possession; Ashley is interested in inheriting it; Thao is supposed to steal it as an initiation ritual into Spider's gang; Walt offers it to Thao to take Youa on a date; given to Thao after Walt's death
- **symbolism:** masculinity, traditionalism, an ordered world, friendship vs. mere materialistic gain

**Examples**

- **Setting 2:**
  **Ashley:** So, what are you like going to do with it like, when … you die?
  (after Dorothy's funeral, Ashley and Walt in the garage) ⇒ **mere materialistic gain**
- **Setting 25:**
  **Walt:** The bus?! That's no good. A charming young lady like this deserves to go in style. […]
  **Thao:** The Gran Torino? You'd let me drive it?
  **Walt:** Sure. Why not.
  (during the barbecue in Walt's garden, Thao and Youa planning their first date) ⇒ **masculinity, friendship**
- **Setting 32:**
  **Lawyer:** "And to my friend, Thao Vang Lor, I leave my 1972 Gran Torino on the condition that you don't choptop the roof like a damned spick, don't paint any idiotic flames on it like some white-trash hillbilly and don't put a big gay spoiler on the rear-end like you see on all the other zipperheads' cars. It just looks like hell. If you can refrain from doing any of that, it's yours."
  (reading of Walt's last will)

## Life and death (religious symbolism)

- **importance in the film:** film begins and ends with a funeral scene (Dorothy and Walt); theme of Father Janovich's sermons and his conversations with Walt; Hmong birth ceremony as opposed to Dorothy's funeral reception; Walt has a critical illness and sacrifices his life for Thao and Sue (dies in Christlike manner)
- **symbolism:** friendship with Hmong and atonement for his sins give Walt new life (although he dies)

**Examples**

- **Setting 1:**
  **Father Janovich:** And some may ask, what is death. Is it the end? Or is it the beginning? And what is life? What is this thing we call life?
  (sermon at Dorothy's funeral service)

- **Setting 7:**
  **Walt:** "Death is bittersweet? Bitter in the pain, sweet in the salvation." That's what you know of life and death? Good God, it's pathetic.
  **Father Janovich:** What do you know, Mr. Kowalski?
  **Walt:** Plenty. I lived with death for three years in Korea. We shot people, we stabbed them with bayonets, we hacked seventeen-year-old kids to death with shovels, for Christ's sake. I did things that won't leave me till the day I die, horrible things, things I have to live with.
  **Father Janovich:** And what about life?
  **Walt:** Well ... I survived the war ... got married ... and raised a family.
  **Father Janovich:** Sounds like you know more about death than you do living.
  **Walt:** Maybe so.
  (conversation between Walt and Father Janovich in bar)

- **Setting 30:**
  **Thao:** How many?
  **Walt:** How many what?
  **Thao:** How many men did you kill in Korea?
  **Walt:** Thirteen for sure. Probably more.
  **Thao:** What was it like to kill a man?
  **Walt:** You don't want to know. […] You wanna know what it's like to kill a man? Well, it's goddamn awful, that's what it is. The only thing worse is getting a medal for killing some poor kid that wanted to just give up, that's all. A dumb, scared, little gook, just about your age. I shot him with the same rifle you just held upstairs. I've thought about that kid for fifty years. And I promise you, boy, you want no part of it. Me, I've got blood on my hands. I'm soiled. Forgive me for tricking you like a dope. […] You've come a long way. I'm proud to call you a friend. You have your whole life ahead of you, whereas this is what I do. I finish things.
  (Walt locking Thao in the basement before setting off for the gang's house to his death)

### Dilapidation vs. refurbishment

- **importance in the film:** street in disrepair one reason for Walt to scorn his Hmong neighbours; Thao's job when working for Walt: refurbishing houses in the street; Thao's job at construction site; Thao and Walt mutually helping each other with repairs
- **symbolism:** loss of old values and traditions; growing up; gaining self-confidence; friendship

**Examples**

- **Setting 17:**
  **Thao:** What do you have for me today? You want me to watch paint dry or maybe count the clouds that pass by? […] Look, I'm stuck here. Why don't you give me something useful to do?
  **Walt:** Because unlike you I'm not useless. I maintain my property, whereas you swamp rats let your houses go to hell.
  (Thao wanting to work for Walt, Walt's prejudiced attitude) ⇒ **loss of old values and traditions; gaining self-confidence**
- **Setting 20:**
  **Walt:** This is for you. Roll of duct tape, can of WD-40 and a pair of vise-grips. Any man who's worth a shit can do half his household jobs with these three things. In the odd chance that doesn't work out, you can borrow something.
  **Thao:** Okay. Cool.
  (Walt helping Thao and giving him tools) ⇒ **growing up, friendship**
- **Setting 20:**
  **Walt:** I just need a little push. All the weight is up top, so you stay down and give me a little shove at each step.
  **Thao:** Let me take the top.
  **Walt:** Naw, I got it.
  **Thao:** No really, I'll take the top. It looks pretty heavy.
  **Walt:** I'm not crippled. I got it.
  **Thao:** If you don't let me take the top, I ain't helping. I'll go home.
  **Walt:** Listen, zipper head, now's not the time to go and …
  **Thao:** You listen, old man. You came and got me because you needed help, so let me help you. Either it's top or I'm out of here.
  (Thao helping Walt with the freezer and asserting himself) ⇒ **growing up, gaining self-confidence, friendship**

## Names

- **importance in the film:** Walt wants Father Janovich to call him "Mr. Kowalski", later he lets him call him "Walt"; Walt calling Hmong wrong names ("Toad" for "Thao"); Sue calling Walt "Wally"
- **symbolism:** distance vs. closer relationship (respect, friendship)

**Examples**

- **Setting 4:**
  **Father Janovich:** Hi there, Walt.
  **Walt:** Listen, son, you're not my barber, you're not a friend, so why in the hell do you think you can call me Walt?
  **Father Janovich:** Sorry … Mr. Kowalski.
  (Father Janovich's attempt to talk to Walt and get him to confess) ⇒ **distance**

- **Setting 27:**
  **Father Janovich:** So, what are you going to do, Mr. Kowalski?
  **Walt:** Call me Walt.
  (after the attack on Sue, shortly before Walt finally goes to confession)
  ⇒ **closer relationship** (**respect**)
- **Setting 14:**
  **Sue:** Happy birthday, Wally.
  **Walt:** Don't call me Wally.
  (Sue inviting Walt to Hmong party) ⇒ **gradually closer relationship** (**friendship**)
- **Setting 20:**
  **Sue:** You're a good man, Wally. I wish our dad would have been more like you.
  (Sue thanks Walt for being a role model for Thao) ⇒ **closer relationship**
- **Setting 15:**
  **Sue:** Well, look who's over there.
  **Walt:** What's-his-name who tried to steal my Gran Torino.
  **Sue:** My brother, Thao.
  **Walt:** Yeah, Toad.
  (at the party in the Lors' house) ⇒ **distance, lack of respect**
- **Setting 32:**
  **Lawyer:** "And to my friend, Thao Vang Lor, I leave my 1972 Gran Torino […]"
  (reading of Walt's last will) ⇒ **closer relationship** (**friendship, respect**)

## Walt's Silver Star medal and lighter

- **importance in the film:** emblems of Walt's military service and successes; Silver Star medal as a gift to Thao (to make him go to the basement and stop him from joining Walt and taking revenge on the gang); lighter provokes gang into shooting unarmed Walt
- **symbolism:** guilt and redemption, true bravery

**Example**

- **Setting 30:**
  **Walt:** I got something I wanna show you. Come on.
  **Thao:** What?
  **Walt:** 1952, we were sent up to take out a chink machine-gun nest. Been shredding us up pretty good. I was the only one that came back that day. For that, they gave me a silver star. Here it is. Here. I want you to have it.
  **Thao:** Why?
  **Walt:** Why? Because we all knew the dangers that night, but we went anyway. That's the way it might be tonight. There's always a chance you don't come back. […]

You wanna know what it's like to kill a man? Well, it's goddamn awful, that's what it is. The only thing worse is getting a medal for killing some poor kid that wanted to just give up, that's all.

(Walt locking Thao in basement before going out to bring down the gang and giving him his silver star medal)

- **Setting 31:**
  **Walt:** Got a light? No? Me, I've got a light. ... Hail Mary, full of grace.
  (Walt before taking out his cigarette lighter and being shot dead)

# 5 Background information

### Korean War

- 1950–1953
- after World War II, Korea was divided into the communist North and non-communist South
- in 1950, the North Korean Army (backed by the Soviet Union) invaded South Korea
- US intervention to stop communist expansion (Cold War era)
- at the end of the Korean War, the country was divided again

### Detroit

- Henry Ford founded the Ford Motor Company in 1903
- Detroit became "Motor City", the world's automotive capital
- by the 1940s, Detroit was the fourth largest city in the US
- at the end of the 20th century, loss of jobs in the auto industry
- loss in population (under 700 000 in 2017; 1.8 million in 1950)
- urban decay
- Detroit declared bankruptcy in 2013
- today, many investments and projects to make the city attractive again, but unemployment and poverty still pressing problems

# 6 Cinematic devices

## Camera work and editing

**Word bank**

| | |
|---|---|
| **Field sizes** | |
| **long shot** | object shown from a distance<br>→ to introduce a new setting (establishing shot) |
| **medium shot** | objects shown from middle distance; characters shown usually from waist to head |
| **close-up** | faces or objects shown from a short range<br>→ often used to show feelings (reaction shot) |
| **point of view shot** | scene shown from the perspective of one of the characters |
| **Camera angles** | |
| **high angle shot** | camera looking down on a scene from above<br>→ subjects seem smaller |
| **low angle shot** | camera looking up at a scene from below<br>→ subjects seem larger |
| **Camera speed** | |
| **slow motion** | scene played at a slower than natural pace → more intensity |
| **fast motion** | scene played at a faster than natural pace |
| **Montage / Editing** | |
| **cut** | transition between two shots, where one image is suddenly replaced by another |
| **fade in** | an image slowly appears out of a black screen |
| **fade out** | an image slowly fades to a black screen |
| **dissolve** | combination of fade out and fade in, one scene fading into another one → to illustrate the passing of time |
| **parallel action / cross-cutting** | alternating showing of scenes that occur simultaneously in different places |

**Examples**

**Field sizes**

- **Setting 1: long shot** of church at the beginning of the film (to introduce the setting/the frame themes of life and death)
- **Setting 15: close-up** of Walt's face while he is being read by Hmong shaman at party at Lors' house (to show his intense emotions)
- **Setting 20: close-up** of Walt coughing blood (focus on small detail)
- **Setting 31: close-up** of lighter in dying Walt's hand (focus on small detail) ⇒ **motifs and symbols**
- **Setting 1: point of view shot** of Walt observing the guests who arrive for Dorothy's funeral (shaping the narrative perspective of the film)

**Camera angles**

- **Setting 17: high angle shot** of Walt looking down on Thao who comes to work (power relationship)
- **Setting 24: low angle shot** of Walt looming over Smokie (power relationship)

**Camera speed**

- **Setting 31:** Walt's death in **slow motion** (to make the scene more intense)

**Montage/Editing**

- **Setting 17: dissolving** scenes of Thao working for Walt (passing of time, Thao's development)
- **Settings 32 and 33: dissolving** from lawyer's office to the shore of Lake St. Claire (passing of time, climax of Thao's growing up)

## Lighting

- in general, rather subdued colours → often melancholy atmosphere mirrored by rather dark lighting
- many of the dramatic, violent scenes take place at night → heightened tension
- sunlight/brightness used as contrast

**Examples**

- **Setting 9:** telephone conversation between Walt and Mitch: Walt in dark garage, Mitch in his brighter middle-class home (emotional distance)
- **Setting 33:** Thao drives the Gran Torino in bright daylight (hope for a new beginning)

### Music

- drums for dramatic scenes with escalating violence (“war music”)
- gangs listen to culturally specific music (Latinos, Hmong)
- title song “Gran Torino” (written by Jamie Cullum, Clint Eastwood, Kyle Eastwood, Michael Stevens) alludes to themes of loneliness, guilt, melancholy, past, tiredness, almost like an allegory for Walt himself, sung by Clint Eastwood (Walt Kowalski) in the final scene when Thao drives away in Gran Torino

# The Ambiguity of Belonging

## 1 Definitions of key terms

### Ambiguity

**definition:** if something is ambiguous, it is unclear, not certain or hard to explain and understand, especially because it usually has more than one (often contradicting) aspects or meanings
**deutsch:** *Zweideutigkeit, Unklarheit*

### Belonging

**definition:** if you have a sense of belonging, you feel like you are in the right situation and/or place, therefore you feel happy and comfortable
**deutsch:** *Zugehörigkeit*

### Identity ↔ Identity crisis

**definition:** identity = who somebody is, what makes a person unique ↔ identity crisis = not feeling "whole", insecure about one's true nature or being
**deutsch:** *Identität ↔ Identitätskrise*

### Aspects of belonging

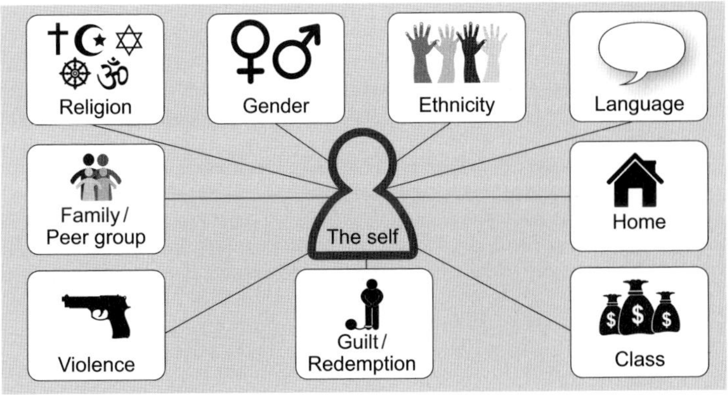

## 2 Religion ✝ ☪ ✡ ☸ ॐ

**Background information**

| | |
|---|---|
| **atheist** | sb who does not believe in God or any supernatural power |
| **confession** | acknowledgement of one's sins (to a priest) |
| **hypocrisy** | pretending to be more moral or more noble than in reality |
| **redemption** | the action of being relieved of one's sins |
| **sacrifice** | giving up sth valuable, often for the sake of others |

### (Christian) Religion in *Crooked Letter, Crooked Letter*

- Ina Ott is highly religious, night time prayer about a "special friend" for Larry ⇒ **family/peer group**

**Example**

- **Chapter 5, p. 98:** "'Dear Lord,' she prayed, 'thank You for Your grace. Thank You for healing Larry's stuttering and his asthma. Please,' she said, and he heard that she was trying not to cry, 'please, God, send him a special friend. One just – one just for him. Amen,' she said, and left."
(Ina Ott praying for a special friend for her young son Larry)

- Larry initially wants to continue to go to his mother's church, connection to his mother, loyalty ⇒ **family/peer group**
- church is the place where Wallace Stringfellow sees Larry for the first time

**Example**

- **Chapter 9, pp. 197/198:** "'But the first time I ever seen you?' Wallace went on. 'Was at church. Bout eleven years ago? Up at Dentonville? The Second Baptist? My momma's boyfriend lived up there. […] And sure enough, they'd just launched into the first song, and I hear the door open real quiet-like and shut and look over and there you are. I knowed it was you right off even though I hadn't ever seen you. Way you come in. Way you wouldn't look at nobody looking back at you. You's wearing a suit and a tie. […] I watched you the whole time, way you stood up and sung the songs, knew all the words, sat down and listened to the preacher, following his Bible verses in your Bible, closing your eyes in the prayer […]'"
(Wallace remembering how he saw Larry for the first time)

- churches mostly segregated in Larry's and Silas's youth ⇒ **ethnicity**

**Example**

- **Chapter 3, p. 51:** "The churches were still segregated if the schools weren't, and sometimes Larry wondered why grown-ups made the kids mingle when they themselves didn't."
  (Larry's thoughts on segregation as a kid)

## (Christian and traditional Hmong) Religion in *Gran Torino*

- Dorothy's wish for Walt to go to confession ⇒ **guilt/redemption**
- Walt's rejection of the hypocrisy of the church

**Example**

- **Setting 2:**
  **Father Janovich:** Right, Mr. Kowalski. Your wife and I became quite close these last few months. She asked that I watch over you when she passed on. I told her I watch out for my entire flock, but she made me promise I'd keep an extra sharp eye on you. […] Dorothy mentioned specifically that it was her wish for you to go to confession. She said she couldn't remember the last time you went. […]
  **Walt:** Well, I confess I never much liked church and only went because of the wife. And I confess I have no desire to confess to a boy who is fresh out of the seminary.
  (at Dorothy's funeral reception)

- Hmong shaman one of the first to sense Walt's troubled soul

**Example**

- **Setting 15:**
  **Sue:** Kor Khue says that you think you've been disrespected. You do not live your life. Your food has no flavor. You are scared of your past. You stopped living years and years ago. Kor Khue says you're not at peace.
  (shaman reading Walt at party in Lor household)

- Father Janovich's development: from rather shallow, meaningless sermon to learning about life and death through Walt's example

**Example**

- **Setting 32:**
  **Father Janovich:** Walt Kowalski once said to me I didn't know anything about life or death because 'I was an overeducated, 27-year-old virgin who held the hands of superstitious old women and promised them eternity.' Walt definitely had no problem 'calling it like he saw it.' But Walt was right. I knew really nothing about life or death until I got to know Walt. And boy, did I learn. (Walt's funeral)

- Walt's Christlike sacrifice ⇒ **guilt/redemption**

**Example**

- **Setting 31:**
  **Walt**: Got a light? No? Me, I've got a light. … Hail Mary, full of grace.
  (Walt before taking out his cigarette lighter and being shot dead)

## 3 Gender ♀♂

**Background information**

| | |
|---|---|
| **sex vs. gender** | sex refers to the biological distinction between male, female and others whereas gender is concerned with social roles ascribed to the different sexes |
| **consequences and problems** | stereotypical masculinity or femininity traits, hard for some to live up to them |

### Gender in *Crooked Letter, Crooked Letter*

- Larry seen as girlish and not manly enough by his father and peers ⇒ **family/peer group**

**Example**

- **Chapter 3, p. 45:** "Rather than his father's tall, pitcher's physique and blond curls and dark skin and green eyes, Larry got Uncle Colin and his mother's olive skin and straight brown hair and brown eyes with long lashes which, attractive on women, made Larry and Uncle Colin soft and feminine, seat belt users who ate tilapia."
  (description of Larry's marked difference from his father)

- Larry's "girlishness" one of the reasons why he is an outsider and why his alleged date is so important to him ⇒ **family/peer group**

**Example**

- **Chapter 7, p. 137:** "Larry looked at the corn on his tray, too happy to eat, a date the next day and friends to tell about it."
  (Larry's feelings about his date with Cindy which makes him interesting to the other boys for the first time)

- one aspect of the plot: (sexual) crime against women (Cindy Walker, Tina Rutherford), Wallace Stringfellow's misogynist attitude (dog John Wayne Gacy, named after serial killer and rapist)

**Example**

- **Chapter 9, p. 205:** "'Sometimes they like it, getting raped. They want you to do it. Carry em out to that cabin and thow em on the floor. Gag em. [...]'" (Wallace Stringfellow's attitude towards women)

## Gender in *Gran Torino*

- Walt's stereotypical masculinity: drinks beer, eats beef jerky, special language with his friends ⇒ **language**, former soldier, solves conflicts with violence, handyman, does not want to show any weaknesses, hides his illness, refuses gadgets for elderly people
- Walt as male role model for Thao ⇒ **family / peer group**
- Walt's aim: "manning Thao up": acquire basic handyman skills, get a job, learn how to curse, ask a girl out

**Example**

- **Setting 21:**
  **Walt:** Be polite and then you bring up something you can both talk about. It ain't rocket science.
  **Thao:** Yeah, but I don't have a job or a car or a girlfriend. [...]
  **Walt:** Just go back outside and try it again. And don't mention you're a pussy with no car, girl, job, future or whatever. Come in and act like a man, Toad.
  ("manning Thao up", at the barber shop)

- traditional gender roles in Hmong culture: patriarchy: men as leaders who should be strong and in control and women whose primary roles are childbearing and household chores and who should be submissive and obedient to their husbands / fathers / brothers

**Example**

- **Setting 3:**
  **Hmong man:** What about Thao?
  **Phong:** What about him?
  **Hmong man:** He's the man in the house.
  **Phong:** Thao's not a man. Look at him in the kitchen, washing dishes like a woman. Even his sister gives him orders and he obeys.
  (subtitled conversation between Hmong relatives after traditional birth ceremony)

- often especially difficult for Hmong boys to find their place in American society because of fathers who are either absent or not able to fulfil the expectations of strong leaders: Thao's insecurity and gang's violence as consequences ⇒ **ethnicity**

**Example**

- **Setting 13:**
**Sue:** Thao is actually really bright, he just doesn't know which direction to go in. […] It's really common. Hmong girls over here fit in better, we adjust. The girls go to college, the boys go to jail.
(conversation between Walt and Sue in Walt's car)

## 4 Ethnicity

| Background information: The American South and race relations |
|---|
| **American South** also called **Dixie/land** (south of the Mason-Dixon line) or just the South |
| includes the states that fought for the Confederate States in the American **Civil War** (1861–1865), i. e. states that wanted to keep up slavery and leave the Union: South Carolina, Mississippi, Georgia, Louisiana, Florida, Alabama, Texas; Virginia, Arkansas, North Carolina, Tennessee, (Missouri, Kentucky) |
| past: slave labour, plantations |
| after Civil War: **segregation** of schools and public facilities (**Jim Crow laws**) |
| **Civil Rights Movement** (mainly 1950s and 1960s) |
| Civil Rights legislation in the 1960s officially ended segregation and discrimination, but de facto there are many areas of **inequality** up until today |

| Background information: The Hmong |
|---|
| ethnic group in **East and Southeast Asia** (originally from China, spread in China, Vietnam, Laos, Myanmar and Thailand) |
| in the 1960s, the CIA (Central Intelligence Agency) recruited Hmong people to fight in the **Vietnam War** (1964–1975) |
| heavy losses among Hmong soldiers |

| |
|---|
| when the US withdrew from Vietnam in 1975, Hmong people were **persecuted by the then communist regime** |
| thousands of Hmong people fled to Thailand, many were also resettled in the US |
| today, more than 260,000 Hmong people live in the US |

## Ethnicity in *Crooked Letter, Crooked Letter*

- **setting:** Southern United States: Mississippi, late 1970s (after segregation period)
- Larry and Silas go to a racially integrated high school, but racism still part of everyday life

**Example**

- **Chapter 3, p. 41:** "In Fulsom his father dropped the boys off at school, Alice climbing out and then Silas, Larry aware how unusual, inappropriate, it was for black people to be getting out of a white man's truck."
(Larry's and Silas's first meeting, in Carl Ott's truck)

- African American Alice as maid (and mistress) of white Ott family (Carl), poverty, single mother, Silas's feeling of being disadvantaged/inferior

**Example**

- **Chapter 5, p. 86:** "He'd known his own father would disapprove. He would never tell Carl about the friendship, but wouldn't it be different for Silas? Wouldn't a black woman be happy her son had a white friend? They'd given them coats, a car. He'd assumed the anger that black folks felt was a reaction to white people's attitude toward them. Yall started it. But if somebody white was willing to befriend somebody black, offer them gifts, even a place to live, shouldn't the blacks be grateful?"
(Larry's thoughts about his and Silas's interracial friendship)

- Larry's racism as means to belong to a group of white boys and as reaction to humiliation and bullying ("Monkey lips"-incident) ⇒ **family/peer group**

**Example**

- **Chapter 3, p. 57:** "*Monkey Lips*, he thought as more books pelted him. *Monkey Lips, Monkey Lips, Monkey Lips.* Then, *Nigger nigger nigger nigger.*"
(Larry's thoughts while being bullied by the black children in his class after insulting one of them as means to belong to a group of white boys)

- mixed-race relationship between Silas and Cindy still undesirable, which sets in motion the events leading to Cindy's unexplained disappearance

**Examples**

- **Chapter 10, p. 230:** "and as they walked along the road, [...] a passing car slowed and the white man behind the wheel glared out his window. 'You okay?' he called to Cindy. 'That boy bothering you?'"
(Silas and Cindy drawing attention when walking together)
- **Chapter 10, pp. 232/233:** "'Son, you got to stop with that white girl. [...] Son, nothing good ever come out of colors mixing. [...] Such and suching like you doing would be dangerous enough in Chicago, but you in Mississippi now. Emmet Till,' she said, 'was from Chicago.'"
(Alice warns Silas off of his relationship with Cindy)

- insult "nigger" ends Larry's and Silas's friendship (connection with inferiority, humiliation, getting the upper hand)

**Example**

- **Chapter 5, p. 103:** "'You,' Larry burbled, 'you n-n-n-nigger.' Silas let him go and rose. [...] Silas looked different than Larry had ever seen him. His eyes now flashed the same fierceness the other black boys at school had, that the girl Carolyn had."
(Larry's insult when Silas is about to win the forced fight for Carl Ott's rifle)

## Ethnicity in *Gran Torino*

- Walt's prejudice: feels alienated in his old neighbourhood ⇒ **home**, likes order and cleanliness (exemplified by his Gran Torino), traditional values

**Example**

- **Setting 1:**
**Steve:** Dad's still living in the 50s.
(Mitch and Steve talk about Walt's outdated worldview)

- Walt's intolerance and racism are further fed by his past as a solider in the Korean War: had to learn to have a low opinion of Asians in order to justify the atrocities, calls his Hmong neighbours "gooks", "chinks", "zipperheads", "swamp rats", etc.

**Examples**

- **Setting 2:**
  **Walt:** Jesus Christ, how many swamp rats can they cram into a living room?
  (Walt observes guests arriving for traditional Hmong birth ceremony)
- **Setting 10:**
  **Walt:** You're nothing to me. In Korea, we stacked fucks like you five feet high and used you as sandbags.
  (Walt threatening the gang on his lawn with his rifle)

- Thao as typical example of a teenager torn between two cultures
- Sue seems to be different: knows Hmong customs well, seems to be proud of her heritage, but also at home in American society (white boyfriend, college)
- gangs seem to provide orientation for alienated male teenagers (Hispanics, Hmong, African American) ⇒ **gender**

**Example**

- **Setting 5:**
  **Spider:** You can't be such a little girl. You join up with us, we'll keep you out of trouble, cuz. (Spider trying to get Thao join his gang)

## 5 Family/Peer group

**Background information**

| | |
|---|---|
| **dysfunctional family** | a family with a lot of problems and conflicts, where violence or abuse often takes place |
| **illegitimate child** | a child born out of wedlock |
| **insider vs. outsider** | a person who is part of a group vs. one who is not |
| **(friendship) on (un)equal terms** | a friendship in which the partners (do not) meet at eye level, i. e. neither/one is superior in social standing, intellectual talents or other abilities, etc. |
| **otherness** | being different from the majority/the "norm" |
| **peer group** | a group of people of similar age, background, status, interests; a group from which one often picks one's friends |
| **role model** | sb providing orientation and an example to others |

| | |
|---|---|
| **single parent** | a mother or father who rears children alone/without a partner |
| **victim of bullying** | sb who is exposed to physical, verbal and/or emotional violence by others, usually in situations of unequal power, like "many against one" |

## Family/Peer group in *Crooked Letter, Crooked Letter*

### FAMILY

- Silas's relationship with his mother: Alice loves Silas dearly and works hard to provide him with better chances in life; Silas on the one hand is dissatisfied with his poor and fatherless upbringing and his mother's seeming servility to white people, on the other hand he often feels guilty for not being a good son and "lacking something" in his mother's eyes ⇒ **guilt/redemption**

**Examples**

- **Chapter 6, pp. 122–126:** "He leaned up and looked at his mother's profile as she smiled, listening, to the bus driver who had one hand on the steering wheel and the other flapping, some story his mother was supposed to laugh at. And Silas knew without looking at her that she would, because it was polite and she lived in a world where she had to be polite all the time. It was a world he wanted no part of. He wanted no part of her. He was already up, backpack in hand, and over the sideboard and gone. [...] 'What's missing out of you, Silas?' She looked hard. 'You ain't seen it that bad. I know. I know cause I have seen it that bad. But you. Up till now you had it easier than I ever did. But now I see what kind of man it's made you, I don't know if maybe I didn't do you a disservice.'"
(Silas and Alice on their way from Chicago to Chabot, Silas running away)
- **Chapter 8, pp. 177/178:** "*What's missing out of you, Silas?* His mother had had to work two jobs plus clean houses to pay for the trailer home she'd bought in Fulsom. Back then he'd told himself she just wanted him out of the way. That was why she'd sent him off. Lying to himself even as he opened the letters she mailed him in Oxford, unfolding the limp five- and ten-dollar bills she sent each week so he could go to his classes and play baseball without having to get a job. He knew now she'd loved him despite his never writing her back, despite the trouble and fear he caused her, despite the thing missing out of him. He'd returned her love by rarely coming home, and when he did she'd doted over him, as if every meal was his last, or hers, straightened his paper napkin and laid another chicken leg on his plate and filled his milk glass or his iced tea so much he could barely stand it. He'd refused to see the truth, that she was starving from loneliness. In fact, he could barely look at her." (Silas feeling guilty towards his mother)

- Silas is Carl Ott's illegitimate child
- Larry's character strongly shaped by the presence of a dominating/ cruel father, Silas's by the absence of a father figure

**Example**

- **Chapter 16, p. 293:** "'He wished you'd been the white one,' Larry said. […] 'You think it was better,' Larry said, 'living with him?' 'No,' Silas admitted. 'I speck it wasn't.' Then he said, 'It wasn't easy without one, either. I used to wish I was you, all that land, all them guns. That warm house, that barn.'" (Larry and Silas in hospital, talking about their father for the first time)

- Larry's lifelong loyalty to his parents: becomes a mechanic like his father, diligently looks after his parents' house and his mother's chickens, regularly visits his mother in care home

## PEER GROUP

- Larry's youth: outsider, not accepted by other boys, victim of school bullying ⇒ **gender**

**Examples**

- **Chapter 3, p. 40:** "Everything Larry couldn't do – spike a volleyball, throw a football or catch one, field a grounder, fire a dodgeball – these black boys could. Did. […] None read, though, or understood Larry's love for books." (Larry's difference from and apparent inferiority to the other boys at his school)
- **Chapter 3, p. 55:** "He thought that if he did a good one, better than anybody else, they might let him go to the drive-in, he imagined telling his daddy about it, Where you going boy? To the drive-in movie with my friends, in a car." (Larry trying to impress classmates with jump off swing)

- friendship with Silas on unequal footing: Silas is socially "inferior", but more self-confident, more popular ⇒ **class**

**Examples**

- **Chapter 3, p. 63:** "Then he moved the gun, continued his pan until he stopped on a pine tree and shot. He levered the rifle and this time caught the ejected hull. It clinked against the other in his palm. He put them both in his coat pocket, and it struck Larry with a wave of sadness, a boy saving the hulls as something valuable. 'Go on keep it,' Larry blurted. 'The rifle.'" (beginning of Larry's and Silas's friendship)
- **Chapter 5, p. 87:** "Because Silas had started playing baseball at school, Larry worried that he was losing him." (friendship on unequal footing)

- interracial friendship unusual ⇒ **ethnicity**

**Examples**

- **Chapter 3, p. 60:** "Silas hesitated, too, then, perhaps because they were alone in the woods, no school around them, they shook, Silas's fingers again enveloped Larry's glove."
(Larry and Silas becoming friends outside of "social boundaries")
- **Chapter 4, p. 69:** "He stood leaning on the gate and saw himself years ago, the day he'd come here. No grown-ups, no teachers, no other girls or boys, black or white, just him and Larry."
(Silas remembering his and Larry's secret friendship)

- Silas's popularity and social standing in Chabot: baseball star, later police officer, but also based on concealing the truth about Cindy's disappearance ⇒ **guilt/redemption**

**Example**

- **Chapter 8, p. 163:** "'[…] By then I was playing baseball. Everybody calling me 32. Name in the paper all the time. And Larry Ott, he was just a hick that nobody liked.' 'How come?' 'He was weird. Lived so far out in the country he didn't have any friends. Never came to ball games, didn't go to the junior prom. Always reading his books. He used to bring stuff to school, snakes he'd catch, trying to make people notice him. […]'"
(Silas remembering his youth and his abandonment of Larry)

- Silas's relationship with Angie: only gradually opening up to her and letting her see behind the façade of the famous ex-baseballer and popular police officer

**Example**

- **Chapter 8, p. 166:** "'Did you ever go out with her?' 'Cindy?' Not meeting her eyes, turning his hat over on the table. Thinking *Just tell her* but instead shaking his head nope, saying, 'Her stepdaddy was one of them white men any smart black boy would avoid, especially in Mississippi.' […] Her radio squawked and Tab came on, wreck over on 201. 'Shit.' She rose with her drink. 'Sorry, baby. I hate to leave cause this is the most you have *ever* talked.'"
(conversation Silas and Angie in The Hub)

- Larry's life after Cindy's disappearance: marked by complete loneliness

**Examples**

- **Chapter 1, p. 6:** "And Wallace Stringfellow of course, who was his only friend." (Larry musing about his few contacts)

- **Chapter 4, p. 68:** "There was a rocking chair with a cushion and he imagined Larry here each evening, the other half of the porch empty."
  (Silas imagining Larry's lonely life)

- Wallace (an underprivileged young man) sees the outsider and potential criminal Larry Ott as a role model to look up to ⇒ **gender**

**Example**

- **Chapter 13, p. 270:** "He used to come around when he was a boy. Larry saw a little of himself in him, maybe. This strange lonely kid. Maybe, to this kid, in this world Larry hadn't caught up to, Larry was even a kind of hero."
  (description of Larry's and Wallace's relationship)

## Family/Peer group in *Gran Torino*

- generation conflict I: different degrees of integration/assimilation in Hmong family ⇒ **language, gender**
- generation conflict II: in Walt's family conservatism against "spoilt youth"
- relationship between Walt and his sons: feelings like greed, disappointment, lack of understanding and interest

**Examples**

- **Setting 1:**
  **Steve:** My point is that there's nothing anyone can do that won't disappoint the Old Man.
  (conversation between Mitch and Steve during Dorothy's funeral)

- **Setting 2:**
  **Steve:** A lot of people showed up after the service.
  **Walt:** Yeah, well, I suppose they knew there'd be plenty of ham.
  (Dorothy's funeral reception)

- family does not need to be defined by blood ties (Walt's closer relationship with Sue and Thao than with his own sons)

**Example**

- **Setting 15:**
  **Walt:** I've got more in common with these goddamned gooks than my own spoiled-rotten family.
  (Walt's moment of realisation after the Hmong shaman has "read" him)

- wrong image of family loyalty as propagated by Hmong gang

**Example**

- **Setting 6:**

  **Spider:** You need somebody protecting you, big man. That's what big cousins are for.

  **Smokie:** Look, I've been there, done it, seen it, man. Back in the day everybody used to beat me up, dude, but now look, no one's fucking with me. Come on, let's go.

  **Spider:** We're cousins, right? We're cousins, we're family.

  (Spider and Smokie trying to persuade Thao to join their gang)

## 6 Class

**Background information**

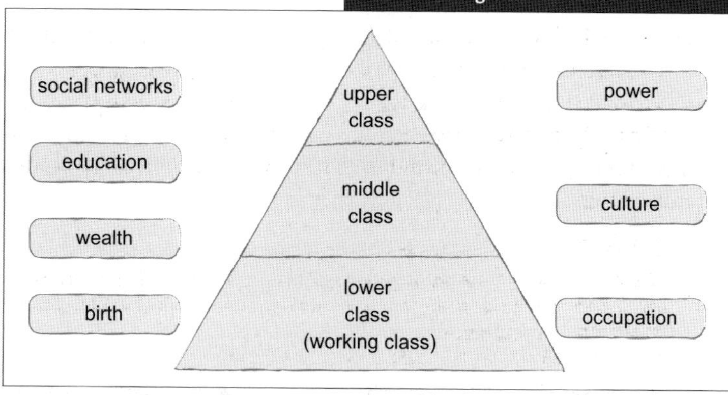


### Class in *Crooked Letter, Crooked Letter*

- Larry is born into a rather well-off middle-class family (possession of land, father's respected job in his own garage) ⇒ **family / peer group**
- Silas's early time in Chabot marked by extreme poverty: single mother Alice has two jobs, they live on the fringes of society in Otts' old cabin; Silas aware of this inequality ⇒ **family / peer group**

**Examples**

- **Chapter 3, pp. 38/39:** "The first thing he noticed was that they didn't have coats. [...] They smelled like smoke, Silas and his mother, and Larry realized where they must live. His father owned over five hundred acres, much of it in the bottom-right corner of the county, and on the southeast end, a half a mile from the dirt road, if you knew where to look, was an old log hunting cabin centered along with a few trees in a field a few acres across, just a little bump on the land. Bare furnishings inside, dirt floor, no water or electricity."
(the Jones' poverty at the beginning of their time in Chabot)
- **Chapter 8, p. 174:** "*Good work, boy.* Silas remembered it. He had felt, at that moment, most acutely in his life, the absence of a father. He'd walked home that night, through the darkening woods, aware that all this land – over five hundred acres, Larry had said – was theirs, which meant it was Larry's, or would be. And Silas, who had nothing, looked up to where the sky had been"
(after Silas has secretly mowed the grass at the Otts' place and overhears Carl Ott praising Larry for it)

- as an adult, Larry's social standing has deteriorated: high school dropout, few customers, has to sell land ⇒ **family/peer group**
- adult Silas, however, has become a well-respected member of society: first his baseball career offered him an opportunity to go to college, then he becomes a member of Chabot's police force ⇒ **family/peer group**

**Examples**

- **Chapter 1, p. 4:** "There he was. A mechanic, but only in theory. He operated a two-bay shop on Highway 11 North, the crumbling white concrete block building with green trim."
(adult Larry's thoughts on his professional situation)
- **Chapter 2, p. 26:** "French was right that Ottomotive Repair hadn't had a local customer – or any customer, really – since Larry's father had died and Larry'd taken over. Silas could testify: in all the times he'd driven past on his way to Fulsom, he was yet to see anyone get their car fixed. Nobody but Larry there, that red Ford. Still, he showed up to work every day, waiting for somebody on his way to someplace else, somebody who didn't know Larry's reputation, to stop in for a tune-up or brake job, the bay door always raised and waiting, like something with its mouth open."
(adult Larry's desolate professional situation)
- **Chapter 2, p. 9:** "Silas Jones was his name but people called him 32, his baseball number, or Constable, his occupation. He was himself the sole law enforcement of Chabot, Mississippi"
(adult Silas's position in society)

- **Chapter 9, p. 187:** "'Well, just Larry, where'd you go to high school?' 'Fulsom.' 'Same as me. When'd you graduate?' Larry shrugged. He didn't want to say it but Wallace waited. 'Never did.' 'How come?' 'I quit.' 'Me, too.' Wallace laughed. 'How come you did?' 'Just did.' 'Me, too. Couple a dopouts ain't we. […]'"
  (Wallace and Larry talking about their school careers)

- "White Trash Avenue": Wallace Stringfellow, Irina Mott and others as typical representatives of a white "underclass"

**Example**

- **Chapter 2, pp. 30/31:** "Silas thought of it as White Trash Ave., a hilly red clay road with eight or ten houses and trailers clustered along the left side and Rutherford land on the right, fenced off and posted every fifty yards, an attempt to keep the rednecks from shooting deer and turkeys in the woods. […] He patrolled through here once or twice a week, different times, keeping his eyes on an Airstream trailer out behind one of the houses, half blocked from the road by a shed. The way the trailer's windows were boarded up, its door padlocked, made him think it might be a crystal meth lab […] Every time he cruised past, the white residents frowned from chairs on their porches, thin tattooed bleach-blond women with babies on their laps, strained-looking grandmothers in housedresses smoking cigarettes, garbage in the yards, clotheslines with sheets lifting in the wind, sheer panties, nylons. In one yard was an old Chevy Vega, no hood, bitterweed growing through the engine block, windows broken, the trunk open […]"
  (description of "White Trash Avenue")

- Walker family: lower class, dysfunctional family, Cindy's wish to escape ⇒ **family/peer group**
- BUT: Silas prioritises his career and tries to forget about Cindy's disappearance

**Examples**

- **Chapter 10, p. 230:** "She went on talking, though, said how she couldn't wait to get the hell out of Mississippi, away from Cecil and her mouse of a mother"
  (Cindy's wish to get away from her family)
- **Chapter 10, p. 235:** "A pleading note in his voice. 'Things ain't so clear when they're happening, Angie. You're eighteen and playing ball and everything's going your way. Then all of a sudden twenty-five years've passed and the person you look back and see's a whole nother person."
  (Silas trying to justify himself in front of Angie)

## Class in *Gran Torino*

- **setting:** impoverished neighbourhood in Detroit whose automobile industry was once flourishing ⇒ **home**
- gang violence probably a result of disorientation, hopelessness and lack of future prospects ⇒ **gender, violence**

**Example**

- **Setting 12:**

  **Walt:** You and your buddies. What's the matter with you? Don't any of you work? I see you lazy show-offs in the middle of the day, slowly walking across the street or harassing women. Nobody owes you bastards anything so go out and get a job instead of pushing little girls around, for Christ's sake. (to African American gang threatening Sue and Trey)

- Walt's blue-collar mentality: has worked in the car industry for almost 30 years, proud of Gran Torino and handyman skills ⇒ **gender**
- contemptuous of his son Mitch and his middle-class existence (job in sales of foreign cars) ⇒ **family / peer group**

**Example**

- **Setting 2:**

  **Walt** *(under his breath)*: Kill you to buy American.

  **Mitch:** Did you see him look at the truck? It's always Rice-Burner this or Jap-Buggy that. Even at Mom's funeral, he can't let it go.

  **Karen:** At least he didn't say anything this time.

  **Mitch:** He didn't have to.

  **Karen:** Well, what do you expect? The man worked at a Ford plant for twenty-eight years.

  **Mitch:** And I suppose that's my goddamned fault?

  (Mitch and his family driving away from Dorothy's funeral reception)

- Thao without direction as to his future until Walt tutors him and gets him a job in construction

**Example**

- **Setting 20:**

  **Thao:** What kind of job could I get?

  **Walt:** Good question. Who the hell would hire you?

  **Thao:** Yeah, I know.

  **Walt:** Aw, go on. I'm kidding. You could get a job, easy.

  **Thao:** Like what?

  **Walt:** I'd think about construction.

  (Thao and Walt talking about Thao's future)

# 7 Language

**Background information**

| | |
|---|---|
| **dialect** | a language variety based on geography |
| **register** | a language variety based on a certain topic, subject, setting or activity |
| **sociolect** | a language variety based on the socioeconomic class, age, gender, ethnicity of its speakers |
| **vernacular** | a language variety spoken by people in everyday situations |

## Language in *Crooked Letter, Crooked Letter*

- especially in direct speech: Southern vernacular which emphasises the novel's local character
- partly racist slurs and insults to mark "men's speech" (Carl Ott, Cecil Walker, but also Wallace Stringfellow) ⇒ **ethnicity, gender**

**Example**

- **Chapter 3, pp. 47/48:** "'[…] Ole Devoid come staggering out fanning dust and holding his head a-yelling, "Call a got-dog am-bu-lance!" Had a line of blood dripping off his nose. A cussing up and down the chart, got damn this and got damn that, son-of-a-bitching shit hell damn. Crazy nigger,' [Carl']d say, laughing, 'sold me the car on the spot, for two hundred dollars cash. I closed the hood and wired it shut and give him a ride home in that very car, him hunched down the whole time, worried bout that hood. […]'"
(Carl entertaining other men/customers in his garage)

- Larry presented as rather well-read through his use of technical terms

**Example**

- **Chapter 9, p. 197:** "'[…] She used to tell us what a good drawer you was. She'd show us your pictures. One of a little truck, which she said was a perfect example of prespective.' '*Per*spective,' Larry said."
(Larry correcting Wallace's use of a foreign word)

## Language in *Gran Torino*

- Hmong family: older generations do not speak English at all (Phong, Vu), whereas Sue and Thao are bilingual ⇒ **ethnicity, family/peer group**
- Hmong gang speak English (rebellion against older generation)
- typical sociolects for different ethnic groups ⇒ **ethnicity**

**Examples**

- **Setting 12:**
  **Trey:** Yo, it's cool, dog. [...] We're going to Red Roost to get some CDs. That place is trippin', bro.
  (trying to imitate African American slang to ingratiate himself with the gang molesting him and Sue)
- **Setting 12:**
  **Black Guy:** You should keep your bitch on a leash, put a choke chain on this whore and yank.
  **Sue:** Oh, of course, right to the stereotype thesaurus. Call me "whore" and "bitch" in the same sentence.
  (Sue's repartee against African American bullies)

- Walt's racist and insulting language presented as sign of his masculinity, "manning Thao up" involves showing him "how men talk" ⇒ **gender**

**Example**

- **Setting 21:**
  **Walt:** Afternoon, Martin, you dumb Italian prick.
  **Martin:** Walt, you cheap asshole, I should have known you'd come in, I was having such a pleasant day. [...]
  **Walt:** Did you see? That's how men talk to each other.
  (Walt trying to "man Thao up")

# 8 Home

**Background information**

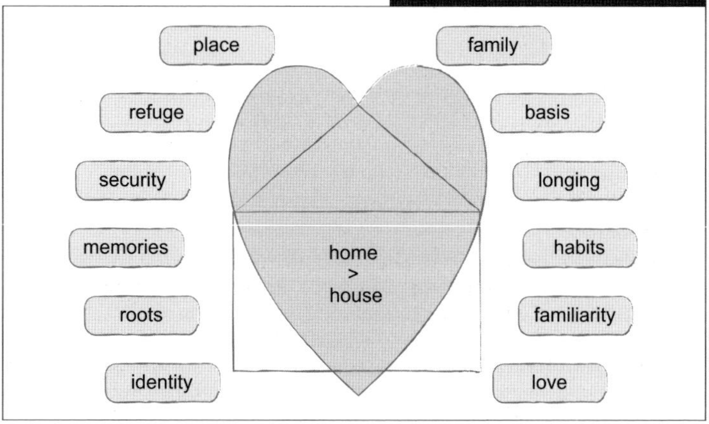


## Home in *Crooked Letter, Crooked Letter*

- Larry's and Silas's local area/home: Chabot, Amos and Fulsom, Mississippi: places in decay, drug problems, etc.
- Silas moves to Chabot from Chicago at 13, returns after college
- Larry does not leave despite being an outsider and having no customers
- they both have a deep-rooted connection to home: family loyalty ⇒ **family/peer group**, "unfinished business" ⇒ **guilt/redemption**

**Examples**

- **Chapter 7, pp. 157/158:** "Larry was called in to his captain's office near the end of his third year of service to hear the news. Honorably discharged, he was moved shortly thereafter back home where all agreed […] that he should care for his mother. In Chabot, Silas was still gone. And still no Cindy. […] For years, after Larry had signed his mother into River Acres, he would wake each morning to the faraway growl of power saws cutting down trees on the acres he'd been forced to sell, […] Soon the land he had walked as a boy, the trees he'd climbed, had been winnowed to three hundred acres, […] Days, he waited for customers, his shop more a tradition than a business. Evenings, on his porch or by his fire, he read. Nights he spent alone"
(Larry bound to Chabot despite his loneliness)

- **Chapter 8, p. 163:** "'I didn't like it at first,' he said, 'being down here. But after a while, after I'd got me that rifle from Larry, and after I started playing baseball, I felt like I belonged here. It's part of why I came back, after all that time. I'd never forgot that place.'" (Silas's feelings towards Mississippi)

## Home in *Gran Torino*

- Walt still lives in his old neighbourhood, although he feels alienated there because of the many Asian immigrants and although his sons urge him to move out

**Examples**

- **Setting 4:**

  **Walt:** Damn chinks let their yards go to hell. Polarski would turn over in his grave if he could see what they did to his lawn. I don't know why these goddamned slopes had to move to my block. This used to be a nice neighborhood.

  **Phong** *(subtitled)*: Why doesn't that stupid, hairy white man move? He must be too dumb to realize he's not welcome here. All the Mee-Khah left in the neighborhood should just move away.

  (Walt and Phong eyeing each other suspiciously from their porches)

- **Setting 14:**

  **Mitch:** And the house, now that Mom's gone, it's got to be a lot to maintain, let alone clean … and you're all alone in here.

  (Mitch and Karen trying to talk Walt into moving into an old people's home)

- Walt's reason for staying: connection to Dorothy/to seemingly well-ordered past, trying to remain in control

**Example**

- **Setting 14:**

  **Walt:** We miss Momma, don't we, Daisy?

  (Walt sitting on his porch with Daisy on his birthday)

- neighbourhood: helping each other, refurbishing houses in the neighbourhood (Walt and Thao)

**Examples**

- **Setting 11:**

  **Walt:** Why do you people keep giving me this garbage?

  **Sue:** Because … because you saved Thao.

  **Walt:** No, I didn't. All I did was get a bunch of jabbering gooks off my lawn.

  **Sue:** Well, you're a hero to the neighborhood.

  **Walt:** No, I'm not.

**Sue:** Too bad, they think you are and that's why they're bringing you the gifts.
(Walt seen as hero of the neighbourhood after driving away the gang)

- **Setting 17:**
  **Walt:** When you're done caulking the siding, nail that gutter back up, I can see it right out my kitchen window, it's been bugging me for three years.
  (Walt making Thao work in the neighbourhood)

## 9 Violence 

**Background information: Gun ownership in the US**

**Second Amendment** to the US Constitution: "A well regulated militia, being necessary to the security of a free state, **the right of the people to keep and bear arms**, shall not be infringed." (adopted in 1791)

Today gun ownership controversial: especially after **mass shootings**

Arguments of **advocates** (e. g. **NFA** = National Rifle Association):
- independence and freedom
- democracy ("checks and balances")
- individualism
- frontier spirit

Numbers:
- USA owns about half of the world's guns
- about 89 to 100 guns per 100 Americans
- only a quarter of the population are gun owners; most gun owners have more than one gun
- 64 % of all killings gun-related in USA (in comparison: 4.5 % in England and Wales, 30.5 % in Canada, 13 % in Australia)

**Background information: PTSD**

**Definition:** PTSD (= post-traumatic stress disorder) is a mental health condition which results from either witnessing or experiencing a terrifying (often life-threatening) situation.

Typical **symptoms:**
- nightmares
- flashbacks
- uncontrollable thoughts

Typical **consequences:** problems in social relationships and daily life due to
- personality changes
- depressive thoughts
- emotional numbness
- health problems
- addiction
- intellectual impairment

## Violence in *Crooked Letter, Crooked Letter*

- Larry's experiences with violence: victim of school bullying, abusive father, accused of violent sexually motivated crime against Cindy Walker (and Tina Rutherford), almost killed by Wallace Stringfellow
- Carl Ott's rifle marks beginning and ending of Larry's and Silas's friendship
- gun ownership connected to masculinity, power, having a father (figure); attractive to young Larry and Silas ⇒ **family / peer group, gender**

**Example**

- **Chapter 5, p. 101:** "'Dead! Well, ain't that sad. And he didn't leave you no gun? Ain't that one of a daddy's duties? Leave his boy a firearm?'" (Carl Ott to Silas before making him and Larry fight for his gun)

- in their adult lives, both men are rather suspicious of guns

**Examples**

- **Chapter 2, p. 13:** "Here he was two years as Chabot's law and he'd never fired his pistol except at targets." (Silas as a policeman)
- **Chapter 9, p. 191:** "'Ain't you got a gun?' Larry shook his head and Wallace sat there with his mouth open, as if he were unable to fathom gunlessness." (conversation between Larry and Wallace about guns)

## Violence in *Gran Torino*

- escalation of violence: insults, threats, physical violence (Smokie burning Thao with cigarette, Walt beating up Smokie, gun attack, Sue's rape, Walt provoking gang into shooting him dead)
- Walt probably suffering from PTSD: distanced relationship with fellow men, emotional numbness, bitterness, recurring feelings of guilt ⇒ **guilt / redemption**

**Example**

- **Setting 15:**
  **Sue:** Kor Khue says that you think you've been disrespected. You do not live your life. Your food has no flavor. You are scared of your past. You stopped living years and years ago. Kor Khue says you're not at peace.
  (shaman reading Walt at party in Lor household)

- Walt used to solving problems by use of violence (war veteran) ⇒ **gender**

**Example**

■ **Setting 10:**

**Walt:** Don't think for a second I won't blow a big hole in your face and it won't bother me a bit, not any more than if I shot a deer. Now get off my goddamned lawn. Believe me, kid, I'll blow your damn head off, go back to bed and sleep like a baby. I couldn't care less. [...] You're nothing to me. In Korea, we stacked fucks like you five feet high and used you as sandbags.

(Walt "rescues" Thao from the gang)

- ending of the conflict and Walt's redemption and self-sacrifice: Walt is unarmed ⇒ **guilt/redemption**

**Example**

■ **Setting 31:**

**Hmong Police Officer** *(subtitled)*: The old guy reaches for a lighter and they gunned him down. The gang said the old guy was here to kill them, but he didn't have a weapon.

(explaining Walt's death to Thao)

## 10 Guilt/Redemption

**Background information**

| Stage 1 | Stage 2 | | Stage 3 |
|---|---|---|---|
| causes → | | ← overcoming of → | |
| **bad deed** | **guilt** | | **redemption** |
| immoral action | remorse | | compensation |
| violence | bad conscience | | atonement |
| sin | (self-)blame | | relief |
| crime | hatred | | self-sacrifice |
| lie | revenge | | apology |
| betrayal | vicious circle | | forgiveness |

## Guilt/Redemption in *Crooked Letter, Crooked Letter*

- apparently obvious guilt (Larry and his alleged crime) vs. hidden guilt (Silas's cowardice)

**Examples**

- **Chapter 12, p. 254:** "'We were friends. Weren't we, Silas?' *Tell the fucking truth, 32. Silas.* 'You were, Larry,' he said. 'I don't know what I was.'"
(Silas admitting his involvement in Cindy's disappearance for the first time)
- **Chapter 14, p. 273:** "'Well, sugar,' […] 'don't be too hard on yourself. Now and again it's okay to let yourself off the hook.' But that was his trouble, wasn't it? Letting himself off the hook had been his way of life."
(conversation about guilt and responsibility between Silas and Marla in "The Hub")

- "nigger" insult as real reason for end of friendship or as pretext for conscience-stricken Silas not to tell the truth

**Example**

- **Chapter 6, p. 105:** "For so long he'd used that stuttered 'nigger' as an excuse to avoid him. Coming back home, rare as he did, from Ole Miss, from the navy, Silas had never asked about Larry. Once in a while as he drank and smoked weed with M&M and their pals, Larry's name would come up. Scary Larry they'd begun to call him; should they ride over fuck with him? But Silas would change the subject, put Larry out of his mind."
(Silas trying to justify his abandonment of Larry)

- Wallace's obvious guilt and Larry's attempt at denying it

**Example**

- **Chapter 9, p. 209:** "Wallace's visits had shown him that being lonesome was its own fast, that after going unnourished for so long, even the foulest bite could remind your body how much it needed to eat. That you could be starving and not even know it. 'Dear God,' he prayed at night. 'Please forgive my sins, and send me some business. Give Momma a good day tomorrow or take her if it's time. And help Wallace, God. Please."
(Larry realising that Wallace has done something wrong, but still wanting to help him)

- Silas's attempts at making up for past errors: feeding the chickens, visiting Mrs Ott, finally telling the truth, visiting Larry

**Example**

- **Chapter 18, pp. 302/303:** "He did just that, came in the room and sat on the edge of the bed. Larry wouldn't look at him, just gazed at the television […] He'd put the box of mail on the foot of Larry's bed but Larry wouldn't acknowledge it. […] 'I'm still feeding the first ladies,' he said. 'Getting them

eggs. […] Need to hire somebody to cut your grass, it's getting pretty high. I'd do it myself but, you know.' Raising his sling. He sat for nearly an hour and then pushed himself up. 'Okay,' he said. 'I'll see you tomorrow. Bring the mail.'"
(Silas persistently visiting Larry in hospital, attempt at making amends)

- open question: is forgiveness possible after years of lies?

**Example**

- **Chapter 19, pp. 311–313:** "'Your carburetor,' Larry said, cocking his head. 'Sounds like it needs rebuilding.' […] 'You reckon,' Silas said, 'if I was to bring this old Jeep in, you might look at the carburetor for me?' Larry took a moment to answer. 'I don't know how long it'll be fore I open,' he said. 'They told me I need to take it easy awhile.' 'I reckon that's true.' […] Larry closed the door. Silas waited as he made his way slowly up the walk. Halfway to the house, he turned over his shoulder. 'Silas? I suppose you could bring the Jeep by here tomorrow. I got tools in my truck yonder.' 'I'll do that,' Silas said. […] What he [Larry] thought before falling asleep was that he needed to call Silas in the morning, tell him to stop at the auto parts house, get a carburetor kit for the Jeep. He, Silas, knew the model."
(Silas driving Larry home from hospital, cautious rapprochement)

## Guilt/Redemption in *Gran Torino*

- Walt's bitterness: feels guilty for not having a close relationship with his sons, and especially for doing cruel things in the Korean War

**Example**

- **Setting 11:**
**Walt:** The thing that haunts a guy is the stuff he wasn't ordered to do.
(Walt in a conversation with Father Janovich)

- Walt also blames himself for escalating violence of Hmong gang (Sue's rape)
- Walt feels "soiled", does not want Thao's "pure" soul to suffer from the vicious circle of violence, too

**Example**

- **Setting 30:**
**Walt:** You wanna know what it's like to kill a man? Well, it's goddamn awful, that's what it is. The only thing worse is getting a medal for killing some poor kid that wanted to just give up, that's all. A dumb, scared, little gook, just about your age. I shot him with the same rifle you just held upstairs. I've thought about that kid for fifty years. And I promise you, boy, you

want no part of it. Me, I've got blood on my hands. I'm soiled. Forgive me for tricking you like a dope. […] You've come a long way. I'm proud to call you a friend. You have your whole life ahead of you, whereas this is what I do. I finish things.
(locking Thao in the basement and hindering him from taking revenge for Sue's rape)

- Walt's act of self-sacrifice in Christlike manner, redeeming his former sins and saving Sue and Thao from further violence ⇒ **religion**

**Example**

- **Setting 30:**
**Father Janovich:** Go in peace.
**Walt:** Oh, I am at peace.
(after Walt's confession: Walt has finally found his peace, in contrast to his state of mind when the shaman was "reading" him)

# Anglo-American Culture and our Modern World

## 1 USA

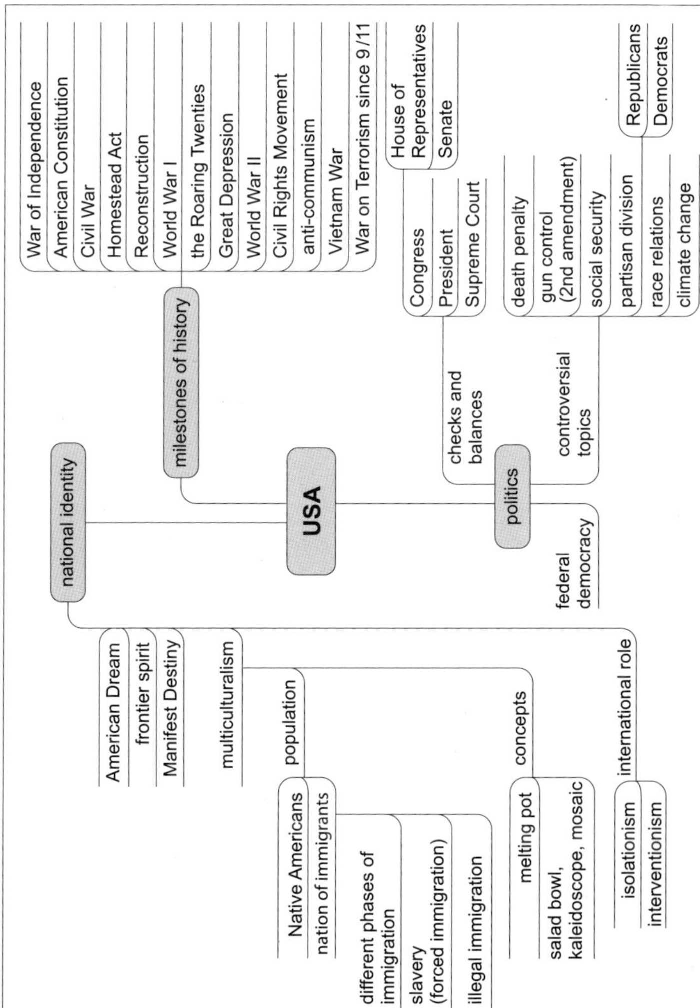

## 2 UK

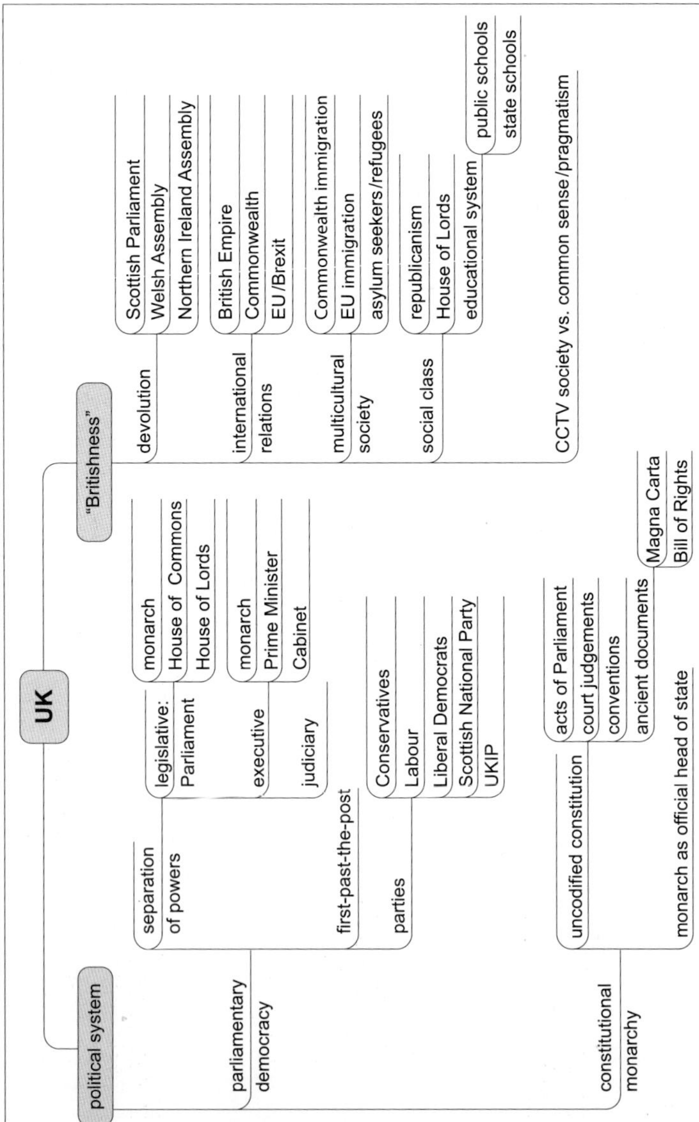
UK
political system
parliamentary democracy
separation of powers
legislative: Parliament
monarch
House of Commons
House of Lords
executive
monarch
Prime Minister
Cabinet
judiciary
first-past-the-post
parties
Conservatives
Labour
Liberal Democrats
Scottish National Party
UKIP
constitutional monarchy
uncodified constitution
acts of Parliament
court judgements
conventions
ancient documents
Magna Carta
Bill of Rights
monarch as official head of state
"Britishness"
devolution
Scottish Parliament
Welsh Assembly
Northern Ireland Assembly
international relations
British Empire
Commonwealth
EU/Brexit
multicultural society
Commonwealth immigration
EU immigration
asylum seekers/refugees
social class
republicanism
House of Lords
educational system
public schools
state schools
CCTV society vs. common sense/pragmatism

# 3 Challenges of our modern world

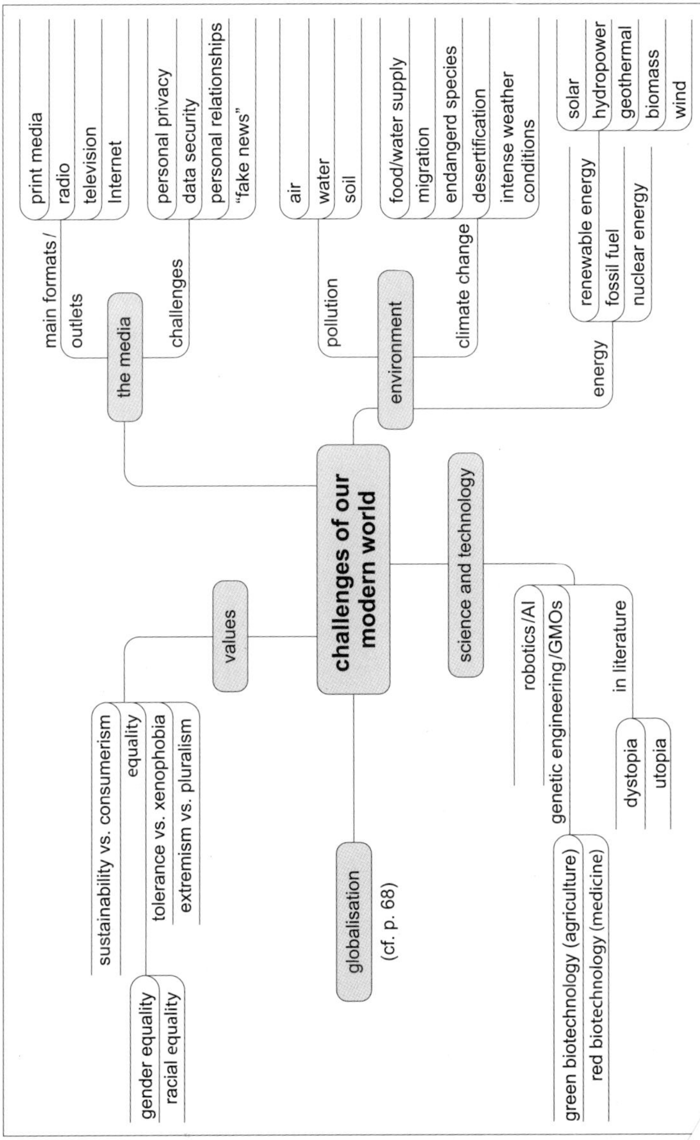

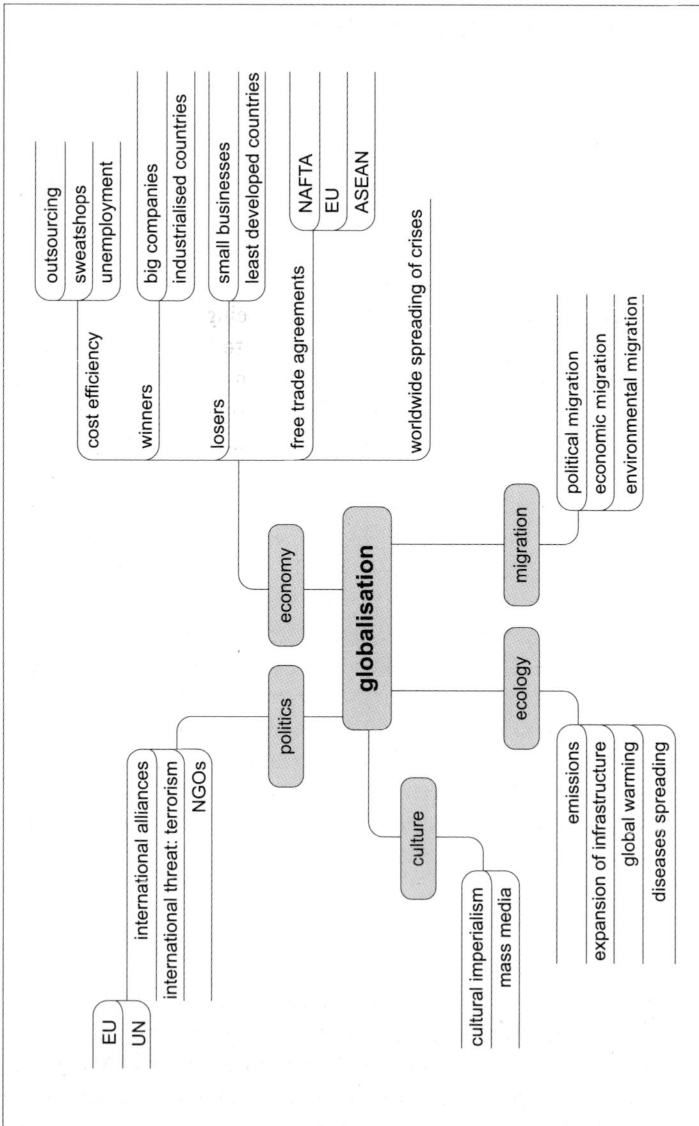
globalisation
economy
cost efficiency
outsourcing
sweatshops
unemployment
winners
big companies
industrialised countries
losers
small businesses
least developed countries
free trade agreements
NAFTA
EU
ASEAN
worldwide spreading of crises
migration
political migration
economic migration
environmental migration
ecology
emissions
expansion of infrastructure
global warming
diseases spreading
culture
cultural imperialism
mass media
politics
international alliances
EU
UN
international threat: terrorism
NGOs

# 4 Glossary of important terms

### 2nd amendment

The 2nd amendment to the ⇒ American Constitution was ratified as part of the **Bill of Rights** (the first ten amendments to the Constitution) on 15 December 1791. The Bill of Rights comprises laws concerned with **personal freedoms** and rights and was a reaction to people **fearing too much power of the federal government**. The 2nd amendment reads, "A well regulated militia being necessary to the security of a free state, **the right of the people to keep and bear arms** shall not be infringed." For years, the question of whether the amendment was to be understood as an individual right of **gun possession** has been controversially discussed. This position was confirmed in a Supreme Court decision of 2008. Advocates of **stricter gun control** cite mass shootings as well as alarming numbers of gun-related deaths (according to statistics, there are more gun-related deaths in the USA on a day than in the UK in a year) as evidence of the dangers of individual gun possession. Accidents spur even more **safety concerns**. Furthermore, widespread gun ownership propagates a **culture of violence**, according to gun law proponents. Opponents of stricter gun control, however, see individual gun ownership as a sign of **personal freedom** and **democratisation**. According to them, individual gun ownership is essential for **self-defence** or successful **resistance to oppression**. The famous mantra of the **NRA**, the National Rifle Association, "The only way to stop a bad guy with a gun is a good guy with a gun", summarises the non-profit organisation's position in favour of individual gun ownership.

### 9/11

On 11 September 2011, the **single deadliest terrorist attack** in recent history occurred when terrorists hijacked four planes and crashed two of them into the twin towers of the World Trade Center in Manhattan, one into the Pentagon in Arlington Country in Virginia and one, which was actually intended to crash in Washington, D.C., in a field in Pennsylvania. Almost 3,000 people were killed in the attack and more than

6,000 injured. The radical Islamist group **al-Qaeda** and their leader Osama bin Laden were behind the hijackings, which were seen as an attack on western culture and the United States of America's standing in the world. As a direct consequence of the 9/11 attacks, President George W. Bush declared the ⇒ **War on Terrorism**. Heightened security measures as well as new **anti-terrorism legislation** followed throughout the western world and the competences of **security services** and **law enforcement agencies** were expanded. Furthermore, **anti-Muslim feelings** surged in many countries despite most Muslim communities strictly condemning the attacks.

### AI (artificial intelligence)

Artificial intelligence in a broader sense refers to all intelligence that is shown by a machine in contrast to natural intelligence, which is shown by humans or animals. Intelligent actions usually involve some kind of perception of the environment as well as **learning and problem-solving functions** to better reach certain goals. Recent applications of artificial intelligence are autonomous vehicles, search engines and targeting online advertisements, for example. These as well as applications in medicine or warfare have opened up **ethical questions** and critical warnings of potential dangers, ranging from mass unemployment to horror scenarios where AI is spiralling out of human control. Another point that is often made in connection to AI is the **uniqueness of humanity** which is devalued when the brain is seen as nothing more than a computer which can be artificially reproduced and programmed to function in a certain way.

### American Constitution

The American Constitution is regarded as the oldest written and codified constitution which is still in force as the country's supreme law. Since its introduction in 1789, it has been amended 27 times. The original constitution delineates the form of government with its **separation of powers** into the executive, legislative and judiciary branches as well as the concept of ⇒ **federalism**.

## American Dream

The American Dream can be seen as a concept of self-definition for the country. It promotes the **ideal** that everyone can be successful in America if they work hard enough and that the country offers **equal opportunities** and **social mobility** to everyone. James Truslow Adams defined the American Dream in 1931 as "[the] dream of a land in which life should be better and richer and fuller for every man, with opportunity for each according to his ability or achievement". While many descriptions of the Dream, like "**From dishwasher to millionaire**" or "**From rags to riches**", emphasise the **economic wealth** achievable in the US, the Dream is also closely connected to values and ideals like **freedom** and **democracy**. Having its roots in the **Declaration of Independence's** famous sentence, "We hold these truths to be self-evident, that all men are created equal, that they are endowed by their Creator with certain unalienable Rights, that among these are Life, Liberty and the pursuit of Happiness", it has served as a pull factor for millions of ⇒ **immigrants** who came to the "land of the free" and the "country of unlimited opportunities" in search of a better life in political and economic respects. In recent years, however, **criticism** that the Dream is no longer alive is growing louder. On the one hand, surveys reveal that the proclaimed social mobility does not exist in reality, that the US is instead one of the least socially mobile countries of the developed world. On the other hand, tendencies like racism, intolerance or scepticism against foreigners are growing, challenging the concept of a country that welcomes everyone with open arms.

## anti-communism

Anti-communism can be broadly defined as an ideological position opposed to communism. In the USA, anti-communist tendencies were especially strong during the so-called **Cold War era** (from the end of World War II until the early 1990s). After the Second World War alliance had broken up, the **USA** and the **Soviet Union** faced each other as rivals for becoming the world's most influential **superpower**. Their opposing economic and political systems, **communism** in the Soviet Union and **democratic capitalism** in the USA, served as justification for the USA to campaign a **policy of containment** and to back foreign anti-communists in their war efforts, most notably in **Korea**, ⇒ **Vietnam** or the **Gulf region**. The establishment of the **North Atlantic Treaty Organisation (NATO)** as an anti-communist military alliance in 1949 as well as the **(nuclear) arms race** between the two countries can also be seen in this context. In domestic politics, the late 1940s as well as the 1950s are known as the **McCarthy** era, a time of anti-communist hysteria which led to mass investigations against real or alleged communists. After the breakdown of the Soviet Union in the early 1990s, anti-communist tendencies became muted. However, the political stance against Cuba and North Korea as well as still existent ideological restrictions on naturalisation provide evidence that the so-called "**Red Scare**" has not entirely become a thing of the past.

### ASEAN

ASEAN is short for the Association of Southeast Asian Nations, an **intergovernmental organisation** with ten member states (Indonesia, Malaysia, the Philippines, Singapore, Thailand, Brunei, Vietnam, Laos, Myanmar, Cambodia). The association seeks to facilitate alliances and cooperation in different fields like economy, politics, military matters, etc.

### Bill of Rights (UK)

The Bill of Rights was passed in 1689 and is one of the most important historical documents making up the ⇒ **uncodified British constitution**. In it, certain civil rights are defined and the monarch's power is limited in favour of Parliament. After the **English Civil War** in the mid-17th century and the following **Restoration period**, which resulted in the autocratic rule of a Catholic monarch (James II), the aspirations of the **Glorious Revolution**, which established the Protestants William of Orange and his wife Mary on the throne, were written down in the Bill of Rights.

## Brexit

Brexit is short for "British exit from the European Union". In a national **referendum**, instigated by then Prime Minister David Cameron and carried out on 23 June 2016, **52 %** of the British electorate voted for leaving the ⇒ European Union. The main reasons for the Brexiteers' success seemed to be that the **"Leave"** campaign addressed issues of great importance in popular perception like **national sovereignty** or ⇒ **immigration control**, whereas the "**Remain**" campaign mainly focused on potential **economic hardships** resulting from a break, which many voters were not overtly concerned with. The date for the final withdrawal from the Union has been set for 29 March 2019. After the referendum, a time of political insecurities and unrest followed. David Cameron resigned, **Theresa May** became prime minister and faces the challenging task of executing Brexit. Potential problems for the time after Brexit are predominantly economic problems, but also political ones, like a "hard border" between Northern Ireland and the Republic of Ireland. By one current so-called "**backstop**" solution, Northern Ireland would stay in the UK customs union and the "hard" border would then run between the Irish island and Great Britain until a more permanent trade deal between the UK and the EU will be reached. Opponents of this solution fear a split between Northern Ireland and the rest of the UK as a result. Consequently, how the "backstop", the provisional solution to prevent a hard border on the island of Ireland, should look like is one of the most hotly debated issues. In a "**soft**" Brexit solution, the whole of the UK could remain part of the EU single market whereas a "**hard**" Brexit would make free movement of people, goods and services between the two custom unions impossible.

## British Empire

In the 15th and 16th centuries, Portugal and Spain were the first nations to explore the globe and establish overseas colonies. As a consequence, Britain, France and the Netherlands saw their own status challenged and started colonising mainly American and Asian territories. After **colonial wars** and especially after the subjugation of the **Indian subcontinent** in the middle of the 18th century and the victory over

France in the Napoleonic Wars in 1815, **Britain** emerged as the **principal naval and imperial power**. American Independence in 1783 meant that the British overseas interests focused on Asia, Africa and the Pacific instead. During its peak time, Queen Victoria's reign, the British Empire covered **almost one fourth of the world's land area** and ruled over **more than 400 million people** (23 % of the world population of the time). The British Empire was described as "the empire on which the sun never sets", due to its large geographical extension. In the course of the **20th century**, however, Britain lost almost all of its former colonies, due to a mixture of partly violent independence movements in the colonised territories and British decisions to voluntarily grant **independence** to them. The handing over of Hong Kong to China in 1997 is often seen as the official end of the British Empire. Many of Britain's former colonies are now members of the ⇒ **Commonwealth of Nations**. Furthermore, the legacy of the British Empire lives on in many of its former subject states' political, legal and cultural organisation as well as in the fact that English is a global language with more than 370 million native speakers worldwide.

## Britishness

Generally, Britishness is the state or quality of being British or showing typically British characteristics. According to popular belief (or clichés), attitudes like fairness, moderation and reserve, politeness, common sense and a distinctive sense of humour are typically British. The governmental position names values like democracy, the rule of law, individual liberty and mutual respect and tolerance towards others as typically British. However, especially since the late 20th century, the term has often been **controversial** because it is exploited to create a feeling of unity and belonging to the British nation, generating insiders and outsiders in the process. As Britishness is often seen as synonymous with Englishness, both the Scottish and Welsh as well as ethnic minorities might feel **discriminated against**. For instance, the "Life in the UK" test, which is supposed to measure the Britishness of aspiring new citizens, is a constant source of criticism.

### CCTV

CCTV is short for **closed-circuit television** and is often used synonymously with **video surveillance**. In recent years, CCTV/video surveillance has become a controversial topic. On the one hand, in the light of terrorist attacks or other **security concerns**, there is a rising demand for surveillance whereas on the other, people feel that the increase of video cameras monitoring their behaviour in public places is compromising their **privacy rights**. Governments argue that there are legal frameworks in place to avoid misuse of data and claim that the feelings of being unduly monitored are exaggerated. However, protests against body cameras for police staff or comparisons to a "Big Brother" society (in allusion to George Orwell's novel *1984*) show that these claims are far from being undisputed.

### checks and balances

A system of checks and balances is envisaged by many constitutions in order to avoid tyranny. It means that political power is **separated** and each of the usually **three branches of government** has means to control the others. A typical example is that of the US government consisting of the three branches **executive** (**President**), **legislative** (**Congress**) and **judiciary** (**Supreme Court**): The president forms the executive together with his **Cabinet**, who head the state departments, these departments and other executive agencies. The president's job is to protect the ⇒ American Constitution and enforce the laws made by Congress. His powerful position can be seen in the fact that he is both Head of the Executive and Head of State. Additionally, he is commander-in-chief of the USA's armed forces, can veto Congressional laws and appoints judges for the Supreme Court. He is elected for four years and can serve a maximum of two terms. However, his powers are not unlimited: The **Congress**, which forms the legislative branch and consists of two chambers, the **House of Representatives** and the **Senate**, can overrule a presidential veto and can even start a process called **impeachment** that results in the president's removal from office. Furthermore, the Senate must approve the president's appointments to the Supreme Court. Apart from their controlling functions, the chambers of Congress make the laws of the United States; they can initiate constitutional amendments and control the federal budget. In the House of Representatives, members from all states are elected for two years and the number of members varies according to a state's population, whereas senators serve for six years and each state no matter its size sends two senators to the Senate. The senators are not all elected at one point, but every two years, one third of the senators is newly elected. The Supreme Court can declare laws unconstitutional. Currently, the Supreme Court consists of nine judges who serve for a lifetime and can only be impeached or resign voluntarily.

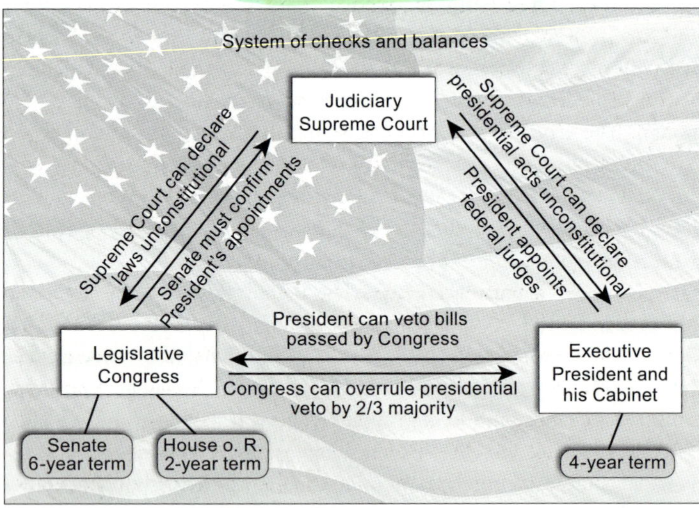


## Civil Rights Movement

The name Civil Rights Movement mainly refers to the campaigns and direct actions fighting for **equal rights for African Americans** in the 1950s and 1960s. The origins of the Civil Rights Movement date back to the **American ⇒ Civil War** (1861–1865) in the aftermath of which **slavery** was abolished (**13th Amendment**, 1865) and African Americans were granted full citizenship rights (**14th Amendment**, 1868). While this made them theoretically equal to their white fellow citizens, in the South of the USA, discriminatory practices continued and were even constitutionalised in the Supreme Court's **Plessy vs. Fergu-**

**son** ruling of 1896. This ruling declared "separate, but equal" facilities constitutional, which resulted in **segregation** in buses, restaurants, hotels, schools, theatres, etc. Unofficially, these discriminatory laws were known as "**Jim Crow laws**".
Starting with another Supreme Court ruling, **Brown vs. Board of Education** (1954), which introduced school desegregation, the Civil Rights Movement gained impetus and organised protest actions, for instance the **Montgomery Bus Boycott** initiated by Rosa Parks in 1955, restaurant sit-ins or marches. Famous Civil Rights leaders, like **Dr. Martin Luther King Jr.**, whose "**I have a dream**" speech after the **March on Washington** in 1963 became world-famous, advocated **non-violent resistance**, while there were also groups, like the **Black Power Movement**, who saw non-violent resistance as not effective enough. The Civil Rights Movement finally proved successful when the **Civil Rights Act** was passed in **1964**, which outlawed any discrimination based on race, colour, religion, sex, or national origin. The **Voting Rights Act** followed in **1965** and secured the African Americans' voting rights.
When **Barack Obama** was elected the USA's first African American president in **2008**, this was hailed as an important victory of the Civil Rights Movement's aims. In the light of still difficult ⇒ **race relations**, continued inequality in areas like work, housing, education, wealth, imprisonment, etc. and renewed protests against unfair police targeting of black people ("**Black Lives Matter Movement**"), it remains debatable in how far the aims of the Civil Rights Movement have really been achieved yet.

### Civil War (1861–1865)

The American Civil War (1861–1865) is still the war in which most Americans were ever killed. The main trigger for the war were economic differences between the **industrialised northern** and the **agricultural southern states**. The self-declared **Confederate States** of America (South Carolina, Mississippi, Florida, Alabama, Georgia, Louisiana, Texas, Virginia, Arkansas, Tennessee, North Carolina, Missouri and Kentucky) wanted to become an independent nation and fought for the **right of secession** against the **Unionists** of the North who wanted the USA to remain intact. **Slavery** became an important issue in the course of the war when the Unionists (and President Abraham Lincoln) declared the abolition of slavery as one of their goals, whereas the South's plantations were largely reliant on slave labour. Mainly due to their technologically more advanced army, the North won the war and slavery was abolished. In the former Confederate States, the Civil War was followed by the so-called **"Jim Crow laws"**, enforcing segregation and continued discrimination of African Americans. Their repercussions can still be felt today in especially difficult ⇒ **race relations** in the South.

### climate change

In a broader sense, the term climate change refers to any statistical long-term change in weather patterns. However, it is mainly used to describe climate change effected by **human influence**, which is sometimes also referred to as **global warming**, one of its main consequences. While there are still some controversies over the question in how far global warming is manmade, there can be no doubt that a larger concentration of so-called **greenhouse gases** in the atmosphere is responsible for it. As human action, like the combustion of fossil fuels or deforestation, contributes to emissions of $CO_2$ and other greenhouse gases, the ⇒ United Nations Climate Change Conferences have been set up to meet regularly and discuss measures to reduce these. International treaties, most notably the **Kyoto Protocol** or the more recent **Paris Agreement**, formulate goals like keeping the increase in average temperature below 2 °C. However, environmentalists criticise these treaties for not going far enough. According to them, the countries signing them only make vague promises and do not offer binding commitments. Countries can also quite easily withdraw from them. An infamous example is US President Trump's 2017 announcement to withdraw from the Paris Agreement. Therefore, the disastrous consequences of climate change, like glacier melting, rising sea levels, extreme weather conditions, destruction of natural habitat by desertification or flooding, are likely to present ever more challenging dangers in the future.

### Commonwealth of Nations

The Commonwealth of Nations can be seen as a successor of the ⇒ **British Empire**. During the period of **decolonisation** in the first half of the 20th century, many of the newly independent countries decided to keep close ties to the British motherland. To that aim, they joined the Commonwealth of Nations, which was originally defined in the Balfour Declaration (1926) and later in the Statue of Westminster (1931). The London Declaration of 1949 described the Commonwealth in the form it still has today, namely as an intergovernmental organisation of "free and equal" member states. The Commonwealth currently consists of 53 member states, of whom 16 still recognise the British monarch as their head of state. Membership in the Commonwealth does not entail any legal obligations. Instead, the countries aim for close cooperation in economy, education and government, based on a shared history and culture and on common values like democracy, human rights and the rule of law.

### Conservative Party (UK)

The second big party in UK politics, besides the ⇒ **Labour Party**, was founded in 1834. It emerged from the former Tory Party, which is why the Conservatives are still referred to as "**Tories**" today. Before Labour became popular, the party's main rival were the so-called "Whigs", the Liberal Party. Traditionally, the Conservative Party stood for **little state interference** and **free-market capitalism**. That was especially poignant during **Margaret Thatcher's** terms in power (1979–1990), which resulted in cuts in social welfare and a decrease in trade unions' influence. However, her "ruthless" style of government paved the way for Tony Blair's successes with the Labour Party, which is why the Conservatives formed the **opposition** for 13 years from 1997 to 2010. During that time, the Conservative party underwent a change, becoming slightly **more oriented towards social programmes and state regulation**. Since 2010, the Conservatives have been back in power, first in a coalition with the Liberal Democrats, which resulted from a hung parliament in which neither Labour nor the Conservatives had a clear majority. In 2015, the party under Prime Minister **David Cameron**, won back the majority. During his election campaign, Cameron, who himself was pro-European, had announced a referendum to let the British public decide whether the UK should remain part of the EU or not. Surprisingly for many, the referendum resulted in a slight majority for "Leave", which is why David Cameron resigned and his former Home Secretary **Theresa May** took over. In troubled political times, she has to try to effect the ⇒ Brexit as smoothly as possible.

### constitutional monarchy

That the United Kingdom is a constitutional monarchy is best described in the sentence that **the monarch reigns, but does not rule**, in other words, the monarch is the **head of state**, but his or her power is limited by constitutional written or unwritten conventions. When looking at their formal titles and functions, the monarchs of the UK seem to be very powerful: They dissolve and open Parliament, have to give their royal assent to all laws passed in the UK, appoint and dismiss the prime minister and other government ministers, have weekly consultations with the prime minister, are Commander in Chief of the armed forces, Head of the Church of England and Fount of Justice. However, all these roles are merely **representative** in function and strictly controlled by the unwritten constitution. According to regular opinion polls, a large proportion of the British population is in favour of keeping the monarchy in this representative function. They point out that the monarch, who is above party politics, can act both as a final control to stop tyranny and especially as a rallying point of stability and unity, particularly in times of political unrest and dissent. Furthermore, the Royal Family do charitable work and are good ambassadors for the country abroad and they also serve as a tourist attraction, which brings in more money than the monarchy costs the taxpayer. On top of its costs, anti-royalists condemn the monarchy as undemocratic, because it perpetuates outdated principles of a ruling class defined by birth rather than merit.

### consumerism

Consumerism is the attitude that ever more buying and spending is a positive thing. Consumer societies are characterised by consumers buying things not only because they are useful or necessary, but rather because they are advertised and subsequently seen as status symbols. Therefore, products are seldom used ⇒ sustainably, but rather replaced quickly by something newer despite them still functioning perfectly. Consumerism is criticised for producing **waste** in large quantities, not being environmentally friendly and promoting **materialism** and **superficiality**. On the other hand, consumerism can be seen as a **sign of progress** with humans rising above the mere essentials of survival and being able to focus on "unnecessary" pleasures like leisure or culture instead.

### cultural imperialism

Cultural imperialism means that a country, which is more powerful in economic, political or military terms, imposes its culture and values on a less powerful country, thereby transforming or replacing its original culture. Historical examples of cultural imperialism can be found in the Roman Empire as well as throughout the periods of European colonisation. In recent years, people speak of an **Americanisation** of many countries, by which the American way of life, its fashion, culture and language is imposed on other countries throughout the world.

### death penalty

The death penalty, also known as **capital punishment**, is a highly controversial form of legal punishment. While the Charter of Fundamental Rights of the ⇒ European Union explicitly bans it and the ⇒ United Nations has made several attempts at a resolution to prohibit it, more than 60 % of the world population live in countries that still allow it. Among these countries is the USA where 31 states as well as the federal government still retain the death penalty. Proponents of capital punishment argue that it is a **fair retribution** for severe crimes, that it can act as a **deterrent**, it **prevents** offenders from **repeating a crime** and it is **cheaper** than a long prison sentence during which the state is responsible for the upkeep of a prisoner. However, opponents of the death penalty cite regular studies that the **deterrent effect is not working** and that government-funded executions are **not cheaper** than prison sentences. Furthermore, they oppose it as **inhu-**

**mane** and violating the ultimate human right, the right to life. As it is an **irreversible** form of punishment, miscarriages of justice are especially grave. Furthermore, adversaries deplore the **culture of violence** that is created through avenging violence by means of violence. Another argument that is often cited against the death penalty is that it is employed in a **discriminatory** fashion, primarily targeting members of racial, ethnic or social minorities.

## Democratic Party (USA)

The Democratic Party is one of the two major parties in US politics, its main rival being the ⇒ **Republican Party**. It was founded in 1828 and is the oldest political party in the world which is still active. Its party programme has changed a lot from being historically rather conservative and supporting economic liberalism to nowadays promoting **social and economic equality**, supporting a **welfare state** and moderate governmental intervention in the economy. Further points on the Democratic agenda are **environmental protection**, stricter **gun control**, an ⇒ **immigration reform** and equality for **same-sex marriages**, among others. Many women, ethnic minorities, academics and young people tend to vote Democratic. Fifteen Democrats have been President of the United States, for instance **Barack Obama** who served as the first African American president from 2008 to 2016. The party's symbol is a donkey and it is typically associated with the colour blue.

## devolution

Devolution describes a process by which a central government delegates some powers to governments on a local level. Devolution, in contrast to ⇒ federalism, which is constitutionally fixed, may be temporary and the authorities of the local governments might be withdrawn by the central government, which remains in control of the process. In the UK, Tony Blair's New ⇒ Labour Party started a modernisation process in 1997, which ultimately resulted in separate local governmental units for Scotland (**Scottish Parliament**), Wales (**National Assembly for Wales**), Northern Ireland (**Northern Ireland Assembly**) and London (**London Assembly**), but not for England, as some critics have repeatedly pointed out since then. For some political parties, however, these measures of devolution have not gone far enough and they demand complete independence for their countries. Most notably among them are **Sinn Féin** in Northern Ireland, whose members abstain from taking their places in the UK Parliament in protest, **Plaid Cymru** in Wales and the influential **Scottish National Party** (**SNP**). In a 2014 referendum on whether Scotland should become an independent country, however, 55 % of all voters wanted to remain a part of the UK. Following the ⇒ Brexit referendum in 2016, in which 62 % of the Scottish electorate voted for "Remain", renewed cries for an independent Scotland, which would be able to make its own deal with the ⇒ EU, have come up.

### dystopia

A dystopia is an imagined future society with **negative** characteristics. In literary dystopias, the authors often **exaggerate present-day negative developments** like environmental destruction, increasing mechanisation, surveillance mechanisms, etc. to make their readers aware and warn them of these social evils. Dystopias often have distinctive science-fiction features because they present technological advancements that are not (yet) possible in present societies. However, they are shown as realistic or as metaphors for already existing dangers and problems. Typical examples of dystopian fiction are George Orwell's *1984*, Aldous Huxley's *Brave New World*, Suzanne Collins's *The Hunger Games* trilogy or Margaret Atwood's *The Handmaid's Tale*.

### EU (European Union)

The European Union is a **political and economic union** of currently 28 member states, although the United Kingdom's electorate has voted to leave the EU by March 2019, a process known as ⇒ **Brexit**. After the Second World War, which had left large parts of Europe in destruction, closer European cooperation was seen as an effective measure to prevent further conflict and establish lasting peace and security. First steps were taken in the economic sphere and consequently, the forerunners of the EU were economic alliances, like the **European Economic Community** (**EEC**) which was founded in 1957. Its six founding states were France, West Germany, Italy and the three Benelux countries. Britain joined in 1973, together with Denmark and Austria, and other countries followed.

From a predominantly economical alliance, the EU (established through the **Maastricht Treaty** of 1992/1993) developed into an emerging superpower with global influence in the political sphere as well. While the **single market** with its demand for the "free movement of people, goods, services and capital" remains one of the union's pillars, the EU's growing influence in other political spheres was reflected in the **Treaty of Lisbon** of 2009, which regulated a reform of the EU's political institutions and aimed for a more powerful union in foreign policy and other decisions.

In the UK, **Euroscepticism** has always been widespread. For instance, the island nation did not join the monetary union, to which currently 19 member states belong and share the Euro as their common currency. Fuelled by economic crises as well as disagreements about ⇒ immigration politics, anti-European movements or parties like **UKIP** (United Kingdom Independence Party) with their criticism of the EU's bureaucracy and Britain's lack of sovereignty gained momentum and resulted in the **2016 referendum's outcome** that Britain will be the first country to leave the European Union. In how far the union, which is praised as a triumph of cooperation and peace by some and as a bureaucratic nightmare by others, will suffer and be destabilised from this move remains to be seen.

## federalism

Federalism is a form of government in which a central government shares the power with regional or state governments. In contrast to a system of ⇒ devolution, in a federal system, the separation of powers is fixed in the constitution. The USA is a typical example of a federal democracy.

## first-past-the-post

First-past-the-post voting is an electoral system in which the candidate with a **simple majority** wins a seat while all other votes are lost. In an exemplary case of three candidates, in which candidate A received

35 % of all votes, candidate B received 34 % and candidate C 31 %, candidate A would win the seat although a majority of people voted against him and the other two candidates, despite being favoured by almost as many voters as candidate A, would not be considered in the outcome of the election at all. A synonymous expression is "**winner takes all**". Criticism of this electoral system focuses on the number of votes that are "wasted" and on the subsequent **lack of representation** of large parts of the electorate. Proponents of this electoral system, on the other hand, point out that it produces **strong majorities**, which in turn should guarantee a government capable of taking action.

### frontier

In its general meaning, a frontier is a border or borderline. In American history, the term "frontier" refers to the borderline between land already colonised by European settlers and the "open land" west of it that was settled mainly in the second half of the 19th century. That this land was populated by Native Americans and these were often brutally driven off their land or even murdered is often forgotten in **national myths**. These romanticise the frontier and the **westward expansion** as shaping the country's character with its focus on freedom, determination, self-reliance, individualism and democracy.

### gender (in)equality

Gender equality is one of the stated aims of the ⇒ United Nations. It does not mean that all genders have to be treated the same, but that each individual regardless of their sex should have **equal rights and opportunities**, as far as education, career choices or political power are concerned. While in many countries important aims of earlier feminist movements have been achieved, for instance equal **voting rights** or theoretical legal equality, discrimination of women often continues in practice, for example when it comes to **equal pay for equal work** or the proportion of women in positions of **professional or political leadership**. On the other hand, **gender quotas** to equalise these proportions are also met with criticism. Furthermore, institutions that are largely based on traditions, like religious communities, for ex-

ample, but also the media often still adhere to patriarchal structures or propagate common **gender stereotypes**.
Progressive gender equality movements do not merely take into account men and women, but also consider other genders, who do not belong to either of the two, and their rights.

### genetic engineering

Genetic engineering means the **manipulation of an organism's genome**. It is an innovative branch of scientific research and is employed in different fields of biotechnology. In medicine, **stem cell research** and its application in therapeutic cloning nurses hopes that genetic defects as well as organ failure and other diseases might soon be curable. In view of an ever-growing world population and the subsequent troubles of famine and undernourishment, the breeding of so-called superfoods is hailed as a solution. **Genetically modified organisms (GMOs)** generally promise better resistance to pests or diseases and could thereby make agricultural production quicker, easier and cheaper. On the other hand, genetic engineering is also met with criticism and raises **ethical and moral concerns**. Worries about the safety of GMOs for human consumption or the social justice of expensive medical treatments being available to only a select few are merely the tip of the iceberg. Reproductive cloning or the breeding of so-called "designer babies" conjures up horror visions of perfectly standardised people and the loss of an essential quality of humanity, namely individualism. Similarly, GMOs could threaten biodiversity and thereby cause a loss of everything natural in exchange for a genetically engineered artificiality.

### globalisation

Globalisation describes **networking on a worldwide scale**. This means that goods are exchanged and people as well as institutions move, interact and communicate globally. While some experts see globalisation as a relatively recent phenomenon, others argue that is has existed for hundreds or even thousands of years, albeit on a much smaller scale. Modern globalisation has mainly been pushed forward by progress in **transportation** methods and especially the rapid advances in **communication technology**.

The **economy** is one of the fields most heavily influenced by globalisation processes. While proponents of globalisation focus on advantages like growth and development, critics point out that not everyone profits from globalisation in equal measure: Big companies and industrialised countries might be able to maximise their cost-efficiency through **outsourcing of work** and free trade agreements (for example ⇒ NAFTA, ⇒ ASEAN or the ⇒ European Union's single market), but workers in less developed countries are exploited in **sweatshops** with inhumane working conditions and small businesses face a hard time in competition with megacompanies. Additionally, the interconnection in finances also means that a national crisis will easily turn into a global one.

Besides the economic sector, **culture** and **politics** are also influenced by globalisation. In both sectors, benefits and challenges of the phenomenon should be considered. Culturally and educationally, an exchange of people and information guarantees the **dissemination of knowledge**. On the other hand, people fear a loss of individual values, traditions and cultures through a form of ⇒ **cultural imperialism** when dominant ideas spread and displace local ones. In politics, international alliances like the ⇒ **EU** or the ⇒ **UN**, pursue the goal of peace and stability through more cooperation. International challenges, like the threat of terrorism or ⇒ climate change, might be tackled best in international committees. ⇒ **Non-governmental organisations (NGOs)**, especially humanitarian ones, also have a larger impact if they function worldwide. However, many problems that they have to tackle are also exacerbated by the process of globalisation. Intensified air traffic and an expansion of infrastructure contribute to **global warming**. Terrorist organisations like the so-called Islamic State frequently make use of the ⇒ **Internet** to spread their propaganda and acquire followers.

Another example which shows globalisation as a two-sided coin is ⇒ **migration**. On the one hand, it is often perceived as something desirable bringing new ideas and input. On the other hand, refugees fleeing from the negative effects of international contact, exploitation, poverty, war or environmental destruction, show that social inequality is not necessarily lessened through globalisation.

### Great Depression

The Great Depression is a period of severe **economic decline** throughout the world, starting in the USA with the Wall Street stock market crash of 29 October 1929 ("**Black Tuesday**") and lasting until the late 1930s. It was marked by an almost halting international trade, falling demands and prices and mass unemployment. In the USA, a severe drought in the Great Plains area compounded the crisis and hit farmers and agricultural workers especially hard. President Roosevelt (1933–1945) and his **New Deal programme**, a series of government controlled economic regulations, helped alleviate some of the Great Depression's worst effects.

### Homestead Act

The Homestead Act, which was passed in **1862**, promoted settlement in the western part of the North American continent as it promised areas of free land, so-called homesteads, to anyone willing to work and settle on that land. This was an incentive for many, including overseas immigrants, to **move west** and thereby shift the ⇒ **frontier** further towards the Pacific Ocean. Homesteaders often had a hard life, especially in dry areas where the amount of land given to them was hardly sufficient to produce enough for a living, let alone to become as prosperous as they had imagined. On the other hand, success stories contributed to the myth of the ⇒ **American Dream** and the land of unlimited opportunities. The other side of the coin is that the westward movement and the promise of "free land" dispossessed **Native Americans** who were the original inhabitants of that "free land".

### immigration (UK)

Especially in the wake of the ⇒ **British Empire**, the population in the UK has changed and become more ethnically diverse. While the country attracted **Irish refugees** in large numbers even before the end of World War II (for example during the **Great Famine** of 1845 to 1849), the foreign-born population from ⇒ **Commonwealth** countries surged after the passing of the **British Nationality Act in 1948**, which allowed almost unrestricted immigration for people from former or current British Empire countries. This accounts for the high numbers of immigrants from India, Bangladesh, Pakistan, the Caribbean, South Africa, Nigeria, Ghana, Kenya and Hong Kong. In response to a growing scepticism of parts of the population as well as politicians towards mass migration, several **acts** were passed in the 1960s and 1970s which made it more difficult for immigrants to gain British citizenship even if they were from Commonwealth countries. From then on, prospective immigrants have had to fulfil **certain criteria**, like having special skills for which there is demand in the UK, to be allowed to reside and stay in the country and ultimately apply for citizenship. With the entry of the UK into the ⇒ **European Union**, the free movement of people guaranteed by the Treaty of Maastricht (1992/1993) has brought in thousands of immigrants, mainly from central and eastern Europe. Another proportion of immigrants is made up of **refugees** and asylum seekers, for example in the 1980s and 1990s, from Somalia or in recent years, from Eritrea, Iran, Pakistan, Sudan, Syria, Afghanistan and Iraq.

### immigration (USA)

The USA is widely known as a **country of immigrants**. Apart from the **Native Americans**, who make up only about 1 % of the current US population, all inhabitants indeed came as immigrants to the country at one point or another, voluntarily or by force.
The first wave of immigration, starting in the early 17th century, is known as **colonial immigration** because then, mainly British settlers came to found colonies, like the first British settlement in Jamestown, Virginia, in 1607. A few years later, in 1620, the so-called **Pilgrim Fathers** sailed to the "New World". They were **Puritans**, a group of English Protestants, who were not content with the Church of England's still too "Catholic" structure and searched for a "New Canaan" on the American continent. Apart from the English, other early settlers predominantly had Scottish, German, French or Swiss origins. The 17th century was also the time when the first **African Americans** were forcefully shipped to the colonies as **slaves**, a practice that continued up until the 19th century.

The biggest waves of voluntary immigration came from the **mid-19th up to the early 20th century**. Apart from the predominantly **Protestant** settlers from central and western Europe as well as many Scandinavians, the mid-19th century saw a wave of **Irish Catholics** coming to the country. When in 1848, gold was found in California, it attracted large numbers of **Chinese immigrants**, who added to the diversity of the country. The predominantly white Anglo-Saxon population felt threatened and reacted with the first of several racially discriminatory exclusion laws, the **Chinese Exclusion Act of 1882**. Between 1880 and 1920, more than 20 million people came to the USA, among them also **southern Europeans** and many **Jews**, who escaped religious persecution in eastern Europe, thereby adding to the ethnical and religious diversity. Due to the massive influx, the first official federal immigration centre was opened on **Ellis Island** in the Bay of New York in 1892. It remained in use until 1954 and has become one of the main symbols of American immigration, similar to the **Statue of Liberty**. It was erected on Liberty Island in New York's harbour in 1886 and has since been a powerful symbol of the USA welcoming immigrants and promising them freedom and a better life. This is famously expressed in Emma Lazarus's sonnet engraved on a bronze plaque inside the Statue which addresses the "**huddled masses** yearning to breathe free".

Up until the early 20th century, the country indeed welcomed immigrants as they were urgently needed to cultivate the land or work in the country's progressing industries. After the First World War, attitudes changed, however, and **immigration quotas** and laws severely restricted the numbers of newcomers. Another change came with the ⇒ Civil Rights Movement's achievements. **Race-based quotas** were **abolished** which is why after 1965, **Asian and Latin American** people made up large proportions of immigrants. Even if the peak time of immigration was in earlier centuries, the USA remains a land of promise for many and due to higher restrictions, the number of **illegal immigrants**, especially from Central American countries, has increased. Immigration reform remains a hotly debated issue, with former President Obama promising improvements, especially for the children of illegal immigrants. President Trump, however, propagates a "zero tolerance" policy towards illegal immigration. His plans to build a wall at the US-Mexican border and to repeal many of his predecessor's reforms illustrate this attitude.

### Internet

The use of computers, the Internet and its applications in almost every aspect of modern life has transformed the world in the last decades so profoundly that people speak of a **digital revolution**, comparable to the Industrial Revolution in earlier centuries. Technological progress has not only been the main driver of ⇒ **globalisation**, making worldwide cooperation and communication possible and transforming the economy and the world of work, it has also affected **individual behaviour** and lifestyles by changing traditional media use, access to information, leisure activities and personal interaction.
Internet enthusiasts praise its advantages in making knowledge accessible to everyone, connecting people from faraway places and facilitating a flexible approach to work and everyday life (for instance, by providing online shopping services, video conferences, etc.). The **convenience** provided by Internet services, measurable in savings of time and money, can hardly be overestimated. However, critics regularly point out the downsides connected with widespread use of the Internet: Being theoretically reachable from anywhere and at any time of the day can put a lot of stress on individuals. The masses of information available can be overwhelming especially as there are hardly any checks on what can be published on websites so that "**fake news**" and unreliable sources when taken at face value present a constant challenge. Furthermore, **data theft** threatens personal privacy as well as intellectual property. On an individual level, many deplore the effect the Internet and especially social media sites have on everyday life and especially on personal relationships: People do not need to leave their homes any longer to go shopping, to get access to books, films or newspapers or to be in contact with friends. While the economic challenges for small shops, for libraries, newspapers or radio stations are easily measurable, **changes in human interaction** are less tangible. Communication seems to be getting more superficial with less face-to-face contact and meaningful exchange. More and more people are almost addicted to their smartphones and they often substitute real-life

experiences with being active on social media. While access to information and communication has become easier, cheaper, quicker and more global, depth, intensity and focus on the here and now seem harder to pertain.

## interventionism

In the USA's stance towards foreign relations, interventionism describes one end on the spectrum of possible approaches, with ⇒ **isolationism** being its opposite. It refers to the country's willingness to interfere in global conflicts in order to promote its own vision of the world and to preserve its economic and political power. US interventionism was especially distinctive in the **Cold War** years when out of fear of a communist expansion, the US government not only financed, but also actively fought wars in faraway parts of the world, most notably in **Korea**, ⇒ **Vietnam** or the **Gulf region**. The proclaimed **War on Terror**, by which the USA professed to rid the world of an "axis of evil", can be seen in a similar light. By being "the policeman of the world", the USA has gained both admirers and enemies. Some stress the most powerful country in the world's humanitarian duty and refer to still-relevant aspects of ⇒ **Manifest Destiny**, like bringing freedom and democracy to the world. Enemies, however, reproach the USA for being ideologically biased and only interested in furthering its own standing in the world with no regard for foreign cultures or interests.

## isolationism

Isolationism is a stance in foreign policy to **focus on internal affairs** and not mingle in foreign conflicts. In its early years up until the 20th century, the USA practised a foreign policy of isolationism, focusing on internal conflicts, like the ⇒ Civil War, or on expanding the country on the American continent. The country entered very reluctantly in both World Wars and only after the Second World War did it take its role as "global policeman and peacemaker" more seriously. It remains to be seen whether Donald Trump's famous slogan "America First" will mean a renewed retreat from international affairs and a focus on domestic politics or rather a more ruthless assertion of American interests with all possible, including military, means.

### Labour Party (UK)

Because of its ⇒ **first-past-the-post system** that favours big parties, the UK is often described as a two-party-system with the majority party forming the government and its rival party the opposition. Although there are other parties, the Labour Party and the ⇒ **Conservative Party** are still the dominating players in UK politics. The Labour Party was founded in 1900 and its explicit aim was to support the **working class**. It was strongly supported by trade unions and the socialist Fabian Society. After the Second World War, Labour won a majority in Britain. The resulting government is remembered for the **nationalisation of many industries** and for introducing **extensive welfare measures**, like founding the **National Health Service (NHS)**. However, after many years in the opposition, the party changed under Tony Blair's "**New Labour**" approach. Tony Blair won three consecutive elections (in 1997, 2001 and 2005) with his compromise between socialism, in which state interference in the economy and ⇒social security is paramount, and individual responsibility. He also modernised the country by reforming the House of Lords and paving the way for ⇒ devolution. However, Tony Blair was also harshly criticised, not only for his anti-traditional Labour politics, but also for entering into the Iraq War in 2003. Since 2010, the party has been in the **opposition**, struggling to find a new strategy that can be successful.

### Magna Carta

Magna Carta is a historical document that fixed an agreement between King John I and the barons in **1215**. As such, it is also part of Britain's ⇒ **uncodified constitution**. Its role as an important document of democracy is sometimes exaggerated, because it **never concerned ordinary people's rights**, but protected barons from illegal imprisonment or unfair taxation. Yet, it was one of the first documents to limit the king's absolute power and emphasise the **rule of law** instead.

### Manifest Destiny

The term was coined in 1845, when it was used to justify the **westward expansion** of the United States and the occupation of foreign territory, like parts of Texas, which were at the time Mexican. The belief in Manifest Destiny to spread the US vision of freedom and democracy is connected with a belief in the country's **moral superiority and exceptionalism**, its role as an example for the perfect form of government and even its status as "God's own country". When the USA alludes to its moral duty to bring peace and democracy to other countries in modern conflicts, similar justifications bring to mind Manifest Destiny. The downside of the concept is that it seems to justify the near extinction of Native Americans or military interventions with thousands of casualties for the sake of democracy and "civilisation".

### melting pot

The melting pot is a metaphor which is often used to describe the American society in which millions of immigrants from all over the world are formed into a harmonious whole through the common experience of living in the USA. However, in recent years, the concept of the melting pot, which propagates **cultural assimilation**, has come under criticism with other metaphors like a mosaic, a ⇒ salad bowl or a kaleidoscope being preferred.

### migration

Migration describes the movement of people from one place to another with the aim of settling down somewhere new. Its subcategories are ⇒ **immigration**, coming to a new place to settle there, and **emigration**, leaving a place to settle somewhere else. There are different reasons why people migrate, for example to live free from war and oppression, to have better employment opportunities or to live in a more favourable climate. Based on these reasons, the most common forms of migration are called **political migration**, **economic migration** and **environmental migration**. Political, economic and environmental reasons can be further categorised into so-called **push and pull factors**, reasons why people move away from one place and are drawn to another. Especially in the case of very pressing political (i. e. oppression or persecution) or environmental (i. e. natural disasters) push factors, migrants can be categorised as **refugees** and are protected by special human rights.

## NAFTA

NAFTA is short for **North American Free Trade Agreement**, an agreement which has been in force between the **USA**, **Canada** and **Mexico** since 1994 in order to benefit the three countries' economies, for instance by removing trade barriers. Similar to other free trade agreements, it is not undisputed, however, as people fear negative consequences for the environment as well as for some workers and industries who might face more severe competition as a result of a free trade zone. In September 2018, it was announced that NAFTA should be replaced by a new agreement, the **USMCA** (United States-Mexico-Canada Agreement), pending the ratification of the three countries' law-making bodies.

## NGOs (non-governmental organisations)

NGOs are **non-profit** organisations that are, at least by definition, **independent from any government**. They often work on an international level although there are also regional NGOs. Usually, they fight for **human rights**, represent civilian interests and have become especially important as a counterweight to profit-oriented economic and political alliances in a globalised world. A famous example is Amnesty International, an NGO fighting for the implementation of human rights all around the world.

## parliamentary democracy (UK)

In a parliamentary democracy, unlike a presidential democracy, the executive branch of government derives its power from the **legislative**. In the UK, for example, the leader of the executive, the country's prime minister, is a member of parliament, usually the head of the majority party. So, unlike the president of the USA, the British prime minister normally commands a majority in parliament. The **British parliament** consists of two chambers, the **House of Commons** and the **House of Lords**. While the members of the House of Commons are elected by the voters and the legislature rests in their hands, the House of Lords, consisting of Lords Spiritual and Lords Temporal, who are appointed or inherit their seats, has often been criticised as undemocratic. In several reforms, many of the Lords' competences were undercut and their structure modernised. There are fewer hereditary peers, for example, and the passing on of peerages from one generation to the next shall be thoroughly phased out in the future. However, the House of Lords can still influence politics in delaying laws by vetoing them. Furthermore, until 2009 when the Supreme Court of the United Kingdom was opened, the third branch of power, the judiciary, was connected to the House of Lords as well. Officially, the UK is a parliamentary democracy under a ⇒ **constitutional monarchy**, but the monarch as head of state does not yield real power, which instead lies in the hands of the head of government, the prime minister.

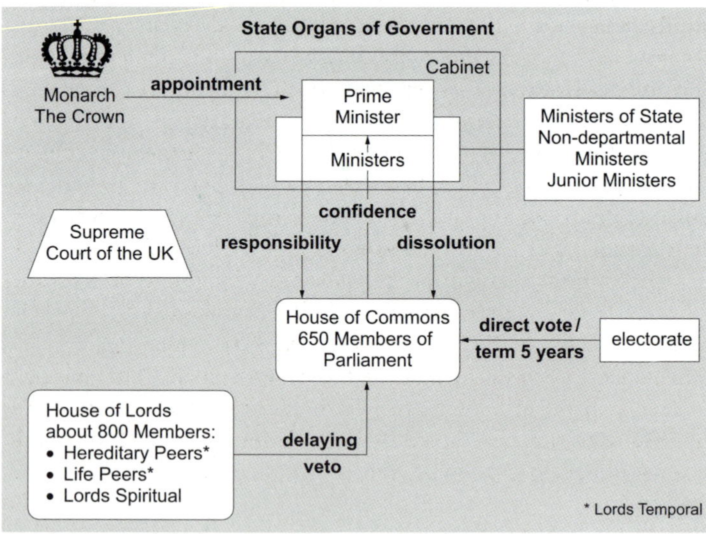


## partisan division

Partisan division is a term that is used to describe the rancour and unwillingness to compromise with which the two big political parties in the USA, the ⇒ **Republican Party** and the ⇒ **Democratic Party**, often oppose each other.

### print media

The print media are among the oldest forms of communication. They include newspapers and magazines, but also banners, posters, etc. Attracting the masses only became possible through a mixture of widespread elementary education and cheaper prices for newspapers. In the UK, for instance, the 19th century can be seen as the time of birth of the **popular press** when newspaper taxes were abolished and the print media turned into an instrument of **mass communication**. As such, the media fulfil an important democratic role because they serve as educators of the masses. Therefore, they are sometimes called the "**Fourth Estate**", controlling the other branches of government and ideally being free and independent from them. Of course, newspaper agencies have to work profitably, which is why it is often argued that they are not really independent and not fit to report on controversial issues but rather conform to their readers' expectations in order to be popular. Consequently, the traditional British distinction between **quality papers**, so-called **broadsheets**, and **popular papers**, so-called **tabloids** because of their smaller format or red-tops because of their coloured headlines, is not always clear-cut. Nowadays, almost all newspapers print in colour or are published in handy formats to cater for their readers' tastes. However, the "seriousness" of the papers' contents still differs: While some newspapers try to boost their readership numbers by reporting more and more sensationalist stories, others attempt to distinguish themselves from the newer forms of mass media, like television and especially the ⇒ **Internet**, through more reliable reporting.

### race relations (USA)

How members of various ethnic groups interact and are treated, for instance in the economy or in politics, but also by society at large, is often subsumed under the term race relations. For the USA as a typical ⇒ **immigrant country**, accommodating large masses from countries all over the world, assimilating them into a common American culture or maintaining diversity in a peaceful and functioning multicultural society have always presented major challenges. After the achievements of the ⇒ **Civil Rights Movement** of the 1960s, optimists claimed that society was now more open and tolerant, and that systemic racism had become a thing of the past. However, critics point out that disadvantages of ethnic minorities still persist, especially with regards to African Americans. Statistically, they do not have the same access to educational opportunities and are more prone to poverty than the white majority. Another point of criticism is the treatment of African Americans by the police. As a result of African Americans being disproportionately targeted and often even killed by the police, the **Black Lives Matter** movement formed – ironically during the presidency of Barack Obama, the first African American US president – and actively protests against still widespread racist practices.

### Reconstruction

The Reconstruction Period is the time in American history after the ⇒ **Civil War** (1861–1865). During this period, the reintegration of the former Confederate States into the Union and their economic reconstruction as well as the treatment of the newly freed former slaves presented major political challenges. The so-called **Reconstruction Amendments** officially abolished slavery (**13th Amendment**, 1865), extended citizenship to all former slaves (**14th Amendment**, 1868) and gave them the right to vote (**15th Amendment**, 1870). However, reality often looked different: especially in the southern states, state laws and regulations undermined official politics. The so-called "**Jim Crow laws**" caused segregation and made it factually impossible for African Americans to exercise their right to vote or other citizenship rights.

### Republican Party (USA)

The Republican Party, also known as the GOP (Grand Old Party), is one of the two major parties in US politics, its main rival being the ⇒ **Democratic Party**. It was founded in 1854 and has historically been noteworthy for being the **anti-slavery party** during the ⇒ Civil War. Today, it is known to promote **conservatism**, **lower taxes** and a **free market capitalism**. Furthermore, many Republicans are in favour of a **strong national defence**, **gun rights** and **traditional values**. With its focus on self-reliance and independence, the GOP appeals especially to "people strong enough to look after themselves", but also to voters from rural areas as well as strongly religious people, like the Evangelicals with their "pro life" anti-abortion stance, among other traditional values. Nineteen Republicans have been President of the United States. The first was **Abraham Lincoln**, who served from 1861 until he was assassinated in 1865 and who is famous for finally abolishing slavery. The party's symbol is an elephant and it is typically associated with the colour red.

### Roaring Twenties

In many western countries, the **1920s** are called the Roaring Twenties because this was a decade of **economic prosperity**, especially in the USA where the financial sector developed to become the strongest in the world, as well as **innovations in culture and technology**. The spirit of new beginnings and a break with old traditions is not only reflected in fashion, music or other cultural phenomena of the time, but also in political changes, like the granting of the right to vote to women in many countries. The hopeful, optimistic atmosphere of the Roaring Twenties ended with the **Wall Street Crash** in 1929 and the onset of the ⇒ **Great Depression**.

### salad bowl

The salad bowl is a metaphor that is employed to describe the USA's **multicultural society**. It may be preferable to the traditional ⇒ **melting pot** concept because in a salad bowl, the original ingredients remain visible while they combine to make a successful whole. Thereby, the traditional melting pot's image of "forced assimilation" is avoided. Instead, different ethnic groups are encouraged to keep their distinct backgrounds because these are all necessary to make up the whole of the USA's society.

### social class (UK)

Social class is typically defined by markers such as birth, wealth, education and occupation. The most general model distinguishes three social classes: the **upper class**, traditionally nobility, the **middle class**, which is made up of so-called **white-collar** workers, i. e. people working in academia, administration, commerce, etc., and the **working class**. The working class consists of skilled, semi-skilled and unskilled so-called **blue-collar** workers, i. e. people doing manual work in trade, industries, etc. As a result of drastic changes in the industries, like technological progress or global outsourcing, the working class is often hit by unemployment and a new so-called **underclass** has developed. Furthermore, there are the **working poor**, people who do have jobs but do not earn enough to make a living. Class riots, for example when cuts in welfare benefits are announced, are not uncommon in the UK. Members of the working class also tend to be among the harshest critics of ⇒ **globalisation** or ⇒ **immigration** as they see their basis of life threatened by these processes.

Generally, the UK is often accused of still being a **class-ridden society** where one's social background determines strongly one's chances in life. For instance, the British educational system with its very expensive **public schools** and the often poorly funded **state schools** is seen as an indicator. Graduates of the most expensive public schools, like Eton or Harrow, as well as the elite universities Oxford and Cambridge are often the ones who also occupy positions of power in working life and their networks with old school or university peers hardly admit newcomers or social climbers. Other critics see the still-existent **House of Lords** or the institution of the **monarchy** as markers of British class-consciousness. While the Lords have been stripped of many of their powers in recent years, **republicanism**, i. e. the anti-monarchist movement, seems to be on the wane according to recent surveys among the British population.

### social security

A welfare state's aim is to provide a basic standard of living for all its citizens, which means that in times of crisis, for example unemployment, serious illness, accidents, etc., a tax-based social security system should step in to prevent people from falling into poverty. The beginnings of the **welfare state** in the **UK** can be traced back to the early 20th century when David Lloyd George was prime minister. His introduction of taxes for the richer and pensions can be seen as a conse-

quence of the pressure newly established **trade unions**, the ⇒ **Labour Party** and socialist organisations like the Fabian Society exerted. Before that, the Industrial Revolution, while making parts of the population immensely rich, plunged others into poverty. Charles Dickens's novels describe the desperate conditions in the so-called workhouses of that time. Many saw turning to crime as the only alternative to suffering the consequences of abject poverty.
The **modern welfare state** originated **after World War II** under a **Labour** government, led by Clement Attlee. That was also when the **National Health Service (NHS)** was founded and allowed medical treatment for anyone who needed it, not only to those who could pay for it. While the NHS and the welfare state's benefits are indisputable, the increasing financial burden social security puts on the state and the taxpayers in an **ageing society** will remain a challenge for governments to come.
In the **USA**, social welfare is one of the most **contentious issues** between politicians of different denominations. According to the predominantly ⇒ **Republican** view, social welfare contradicts the American ideal of self-reliance and being responsible for one's own fate. Although ⇒ **Democratic** President Johnson laid the foundations of a social security system in the 1960s, Republican presidents have ever since tried to erode or stop future developments, like Trump's resistance against his predecessor Obama's 2010 Affordable Care Act ("**ObamaCare**") shows. Up until today, the USA remains the only major industrial state without a nationwide consistent health insurance programme.

### sustainability

Sustainability is one of the buzz words of modern times, especially with regards to the **environment**. More and more frequently, it is also used to describe **social** aspects and a climate of general satisfaction, in contrast to the exploitation of many for the profits of a few. A sustainable lifestyle is well able to function in the long run. Therefore, political or economic decisions should be taken with the **future** and the interconnectedness of all living organisms and ecosystems in mind.

This attitude is directed against a climate of waste and fast profits, which ignores future repercussions of present-day actions.

### UN (United Nations)

The United Nations organisation is the most powerful **intergovernmental organisation** in the world. It was founded after the Second World War with the express intention to improve international cooperation and thereby prevent further wars. Besides **peacekeeping** and rules for **international cooperation**, the UN's focus is on human rights as well as on ⇒ **sustainability** and **environmentally friendly development** and prosperity for all nations. It has grown from 51 member states when it was founded in 1945 to more than 190 member states today. The main organs of the UN are the General Assembly, the Security Council, the Economic and Social Council, the UN Secretariat and the International Court of Justice.

### uncodified constitution (UK)

In contrast to a codified constitution, which is written down in a single document, the UK's constitution is uncodified because there is not one single point of reference, but the constitutional rights rest on **statute law** (all acts which are passed by Parliament), **common law** (decisions in court), **parliamentary conventions** and **historical documents**. The UK's constitution is sometimes called an unwritten one although this term is strictly speaking not precise enough. The laws, decisions and conventions that form the UK constitution might exist in written form, but they are not collected in a single document. This is a striking example of Parliament's powerful position, which is also expressed in the term **parliamentary sovereignty**: Acts of Parliament are the supreme source of law in the UK and thereby Parliament can quite easily and indeed does constantly change the constitution.

### utopia

Literally, utopia means "no-place". In literature, a utopia is an imagined, non-existent society where living conditions are perfect. However, as perfection is closely connected to ideology and what is considered perfect may vary from individual to individual, any utopia can easily be turned into its opposite, a ⇒ **dystopia**, where uniform values are indiscriminately applied to everyone.

### Vietnam War

The USA's involvement in the Vietnam War must be seen in the wider context of the country's ⇒ **anti-communist** stance and its fear of communism spreading throughout the world. After the First Indochina War between Vietnam and France had ended in 1954, the country was divided into a North and a South Vietnamese part. This partition was supposed to be provisional with national elections and a reunification announced. However, the regime of **South Vietnam** refused to hold elections for fear of the **Communist North** becoming too powerful. The conflict finally turned into military quarrels in which the USA supported South Vietnam by sending them weapons and finally even deploying ground troops to the country in 1964. The Vietnam War provoked **massive worldwide protests** and badly tarnished the US reputation in their own country as well as abroad. Both the justification for entering into the war and the cruel warfare itself as well as the targeting of civilians were heavily criticised. For instance, the US forces used chemicals like "**Agent Orange**" to defoliate forests and undermine the Communist Vietcong's guerrilla tactics. Up to this day, these chemicals continue to have health impacts on millions of Vietnamese people. Finally, the US involvement was also ineffective and after the government had to admit their defeat in 1975, the war ended with North Vietnam taking over control of the country. The Vietnam War is still perceived as a traumatic watershed in the USA's military history because of the loss of human life, money and self-confidence it entailed for the country.

### War of Independence

The War of Independence (1775–1783) was fought between the UK and its 13 American colonies, which after their independence became the United States of America. The war resulted from an ongoing conflict between the mother country and its colonists, who felt misrepresented and oppressed. The famous slogan, "**no taxation without re-**

**presentation**", summarises this attitude well: the colonists felt that they were only exploited to serve the British Crown's interests, but were never consulted and had no say in how they wished to be governed. Several incidents of insurrection, like the **Boston Tea Party** in 1773, for instance, when colonists threw tea overboard of ships of the East India Company to protest tax laws, were met not with concessions or a willingness to cooperate and compromise, but rather with ever more repressive laws. Armed conflict resulted, which the colonists under leadership of George Washington as their commander and with the support of French troops finally won in 1783. George Washington also became the first president of the independent democratic United States of America. In the midst of the war, on 4 July 1776, the **Declaration of Independence** was issued. Its world-famous second sentence, "We hold these truths to be self-evident, that all men are created equal, that they are endowed by their Creator with certain unalienable Rights, that among these are Life, Liberty, and the pursuit of Happiness", focuses on human rights and the equality of all human beings. Democracy and freedom should result as natural consequences of this equality. However, in 1776, the principle of equality did not apply to women nor to people who were not white. Still, the Declaration of Independence has served as an ideal to aspire to and a model to copy by people and governments throughout the world.

### War on Terrorism

The War on Terrorism was announced by President George W. Bush immediately after the ⇒ **9/11-attacks**. Since then, several wars, predominantly those in Iraq (2003–2011) and Afghanistan (starting in 2001), have unofficially been called Wars on Terror. Although Obama declared the War on Terror over in 2013, renewed military action against the so-called Islamic State terrorists as well as a continuing military presence in Afghanistan to fight the Taliban could still be called Wars on Terror. However, the term itself has never been undisputed and the wars fought on its basis have been highly controversial. **Terrorism** itself is very hard to define. In one potential definition, it comprises unlawful acts of violence that are intentionally directed at civilians to create fear and confusion. These are often perpetrated by radical religiously or politically motivated groups. As a consequence of this rather vague and, as some point out, subjective definition, the justification of fighting terrorism can be used as a pretext to pursue almost any military or political goals because there is no clear-cut enemy against whom to direct the aggressions. Additionally, waging war seems to be an ineffective means against terrorism because by harming and potentially destroying whole countries in retribution for terrorist attacks, the breeding ground on which terrorism flourishes only becomes larger. Other criticism concerns the fact that governments committed to fight terrorism have also reduced civil liberties in the process and, on the pretext of enhancing security, have turned into surveillance societies.